James Foster Wadmore

Some Account of the History and Antiquity of the Worshipful Company of Skinners, London

James Foster Wadmore

Some Account of the History and Antiquity of the Worshipful Company of Skinners, London

ISBN/EAN: 9783743419001

Manufactured in Europe, USA, Canada, Australia, Japa

Cover: Foto ©ninafisch / pixelio.de

Manufactured and distributed by brebook publishing software (www.brebook.com)

James Foster Wadmore

Some Account of the History and Antiquity of the Worshipful Company of Skinners, London

SOME ACCOUNT OF

THE HISTORY AND ANTIQUITY

OF THE

WORSHIPFUL COMPANY

OF

SKINNERS, LONDON.

BY

JAMES FOSTER WADMORE,
CITIZEN AND SKINNER, A.R.I.B.A., HON. LOCAL SEC., K.A.S., &c., &c.

PUBLISHED IN THE TRANSACTIONS OF THE LONDON AND MIDDLESEX
ARCHÆOLOGICAL SOCIETY, AND

PRINTED BY J. B. NICHOLS AND SONS, 25, PARLIAMENT STREET.

1876.

PREFACE.

The following pages have grown out of a paper which was read at a Meeting of the London and Middlesex Archæological Society, held at Skinners' Hall on Tuesday, the 28th day of April, 1874.

The aim of the paper was to supply concisely and graphically a history of the Company, which should contain fresh matters of interest, not hitherto collected or published, as for instance : Some account of the early illuminated Court Books; Of the rebuilding of the Hall; Of the Company's Barge; and, Of the various illustrious Members of the Company who in a period of nearly five hundred and fifty years have filled the office of Lord Mayor in the City of London. To this is added a short account of the connection of the Company with the plantation in the Province of Ulster, set on foot by James I. 1609.

Those who desire to obtain further information of the Worshipful Company of Skinners will do well to consult Herbert's History of the Twelve great City Companies, published in 8vo., A.D. 1836.

The author's best thanks are due for the kind aid and assistance afforded by John E. Price, Esq., F.S.A.; Major Heales, F.S.A.; G. E. A. Cokayne, Esq., M.A., F.S.A., Lancaster Herald ; Alfred White, Esq., F.S.A.; John de Havilland, Esq., F.S.A., York Herald; W. H. Overall, Esq., F.S.A., Librarian to the Corporation of London ; E. J. Sage, Esq.; and also G. R. French, Esq. for the loan of the illustrations and descriptions of the Company's plate exhibited at Ironmongers' Hall 1861.

CONTENTS.

	PAGE
General History of the Skinners' Company	1 to 12
Fraternity of Corpus Christi	13 „ 20
Fraternity of Our Lady	20 „ 29
Skinners' Hall	30 „ 32
Skinners' Barge	33 „ 38
City Pageants of Illustrious Members	39 „ 42

LORD MAYORS OF THE CITY OF LONDON.

Sir Thomas Legge	43
Adam of Bury	44
Sir Henry Barton	44
Sir William Gregory	45
Sir Thomas Oldgrave	45
Sir William Martin	46
Sir Thomas Mirfine	47
Sir John Champneis	47
Sir Andrew Judde	48
Sir Richard Dobbes	54
Sir Wolstan Dixie	56
Sir Stephen Slaney	57
Sir Richard Saltonstall	58
Sir William Cokayne	59
Sir Richard Dean	62
Sir Robert Tichborne	62
Sir Richard Chiverton	68
Sir Anthony Bateman	68
Sir George Waterman	68
Sir Thomas Pilkington	68
Sir Humphrey Edwin	73

	PAGE
Sir George Merrtins	74
Sir Charles Asgill	75
Sir Robert Kite	75

BEQUESTS.

Mr. Thomas Hunt	77
Mr. Lawrence Atwell	77
Sir James Lancaster	78
Sir Thomas Smith	78
John Meredith	78
William Stoddart	78
Sir Andrew Judd	48, 53
Sir Wolstan Dixie	56
Manor of Pellipar	79

THE MANOR OF PELLIPAR.

Connection of Skinners with Ireland	79
The Market Town of Dungiven	81
Dolmen near Dungiven	82
Tomb of Covey na Gall	83

SCHEDULE OF PLATE

83

SOME ACCOUNT OF THE HISTORY AND ANTIQUITIES OF

THE WORSHIPFUL COMPANY OF SKINNERS, LONDON.

BY J. F. WADMORE, A.R.I.B.A. AND HON. LOCAL SEC. K.A.S.

From the time that God clothed our first parents with coats of skins to the present time, skins, or furs as we now call them, have been used.

The preparation of skins was in the time of Moses well understood, and must have been extensively practised, as we find them employed in the covering of the Tabernacle in the wilderness,[1] which is described as protected with rams' skins, dyed red, and badgers' skins.

Julius Cæsar in his Commentaries describes the Britons as "pellibus vestiti."[2] In Saxon times skins continued to be largely used by the inhabitants of the country generally, but, as regards the origin of the practice of the dealers in skins associating themselves as a guild, we know but little. As the town populations increased Saxon guilds or Fridborges, afterwards called Frankpledges, came gradually into use; but these appear to have been more or less of a religious character, as we find that originally a guild consisted of thirteen members only, one principal and twelve associates, in imitation of the numbers chosen by Our Saviour, with one sister, however, who was added to represent the Blessed Virgin Mary.[3]

---

[1] Exod. xxvi. 14. [2] Cæsar, lv. c. xiv.
[3] Herbert's *Livery Companies*, i. 3. See also, The Ordinances of some Secular Guilds of London, by Henry Charles Coote, F.S.A., published in the Transactions of the London and Middlesex Archæological Society, vol. iv. part I.

Guilds increased both in numbers and importance under the Normans, and the Skinners are mentioned as a trade-guild as far back as the thirteenth year of Edward II. A.D. 1319. The earlier licences to hold property in mortmain are distinctly recognised and confirmed in charters granted by Edward III. to the Goldsmiths, the Skinners, and the Merchant Taylors, and in like manner in the charters granted by him subsequently in the twenty-seventh, twenty-eighth, and thirty-seventh years of his reign, to the Grocers, the Fishmongers, Drapers, Salters, and Vintners.[1] The charter of Edward is addressed to his beloved men of the city of London, called Skinners. That so many charters should have been granted is perhaps to be accounted for by the fact " that Edward,[2] following the example of his father, felt the necessity for summoning a commercial Parliament, apparently more numerous than the National Parliament itself, to discuss questions of trade, and to endeavour to settle the differences between capital and labour;" the disputes of which had led to so terrible a result, in the frightful depopulation of the country by the plague[3] known as the Black Death. This, together with the war which broke out between England and Scotland, rendered it necessary that the king should appeal for assistance to his faithful subjects, not only in the city of London, but in forty-two other cities or towns, for the raising of men and horse, for which latter a sum of from 30s. to 40s. was allowed.[4]

The Skinners were now (A.D. 1339) a powerful Company, jealous of their privileges, which soon brought them into collision with the Fishmongers, an equally honourable and ancient Company.[5] From 1412 to 1422 the rage for precedency was carried to the greatest excess, and it is related that in the time of Henry V. two ladies named Grange and Trussel were so outrageous as to have carried the quarrel into the church at St. Dunstan's-in-the-East, whereon their husbands interfered and drew their swords, and in the mêlée Petwardin, a Fishmonger, was slain and several others wounded; for this they were excommunicated until submission was made to the Church, and satisfaction given to the widow. Chroniclers state that the contest produced a

[1] Herbert, i. 25. A.D. 1327.
[2] *The Life and Times of Edward III.* by W. Longman, p. 4.
[3] *Ibid.* p. 5.
[4] *Edward III.* Longman ; Rymer's *Fœdera*, i. 226.
[5] Herbert, p. 306.

skirmish and a riot, which the magistracy endeavoured to appease, and seized some of the offenders; they were however rescued by Thomas Hansart and John le Brewer, who illused the mayor (Henry Darcie) and wounded some of his officers. Hansart and Brewer were apprehended, tried, and condemned at Guildhall, and afterwards executed in Cheapside; which well-timed severity we are informed was so much approved of by the King that he granted the magistrates an indemnification for their conduct.

Nor were such disturbances at all unusual in those times. Stowe[1] tells us that in the first year of the reign of Edward III. the bakers, tavern-keepers, millers, cooks, poulterers, fishmongers, butchers, brewers, cornchandlers, and divers other trades and misteries, together with the loose sort of people called malefactors, were the chief mischief makers in the tumults, who broke open citizens' houses and spoiled their goods, imprisoned their persons, wounding some and slaying others, so that the King more than once called on the mayor and sheriffs to suppress this evil and organize a city watch. These tumults appear, however, to have continued even up to the time of Richard III.

In the thirty-seventh year of Edward III's reign (A.D. 1364) the Skinners, Drapers, and Fishmongers contributed the sum of 40l. in aid of the war in France.

In 1395, the Skinners, who had previously been divided into two brotherhoods, one at St. Mary Spital[2] and the other at St. Mary Bethlem,[3] were united under Richard II.

[1] Strype's *Stowe*, ii. 255.
[2] On the east side of the north end of Bishopsgate Street (Pennant, ii. 165) stood the priory and hospital of St. Mary Spittle, founded in 1197 by Walter Brune, sheriff of London, and Rosia his wife, for canons regular of the order of St. Augustine. It was noted for its pulpit cross, at which a preacher was wont to deliver a sermon, consolidated out of four others which had been preached at St. Paul's Cross on Good Friday and the Monday, Tuesday, and Wednesday in Easter week; and then to give a sermon of his own. At all which sermons the mayor and aldermen were to attend, dressed on each occasion in different coloured robes. This custom continued till the destruction of Church government in the civil wars of the last century. At the Dissolution here were found not fewer than a hundred and fourscore beds, well furnished for the reception of the poor.
[3] Between Bishopsgate and Moorfields (*Ibid.* ii. 161) stood the hospital of St. Mary of Bethlehem, founded by Simon Fitz-Mary, sheriff of London in 1247, for a prior, canons, brethren, and sisters of a peculiar order, subject to the

In the order for setting a watch on the Vigil of St. Peter and St. Paul, 6 Edward IV., the Skinners rank as sixth amongst the first twelve Companies.[1]

In the first year of the reign of Richard III. (1483) they stand seventh,[2] and at his coronation John Pasmer, Pelliparius, is named as chief butler in the deputation from the twelve Companies who are associated with the Lord Mayor.[3]

visitation of the Bishop of Bethlehem. They were to be dressed in a black habit, and distinguished by a star on their breast. In 1403 most of the houses belonging to this hospital were alienated, and only the master left, who did not wear the habit of the order.

[1] Herbert, p. 307.
[2] They ranked seventh in the Arti Maggiori of Florence. History of the Republic by Capponi.
[3] At the coronation of George IV. the late Mr. John Moore, a respected member of the Company, performed the same office, as the elegant rosewater-dish used on the occasion, &c., presented by him to the Company, records. (Stowe, Appendix, cap. iii. p. 16, Guildhall Library, K, fo. 17 *a*, 8 Hen. VI. lib. 1. fo. 191 *a*, and 6).

Coronatio Domini Richardi Tertii et Dominæ Annæ Consortis suæ.

This ancient custom is thus alluded to in the Pleas concerning the city of London, held at the Tower, before Will'm of York, Provost of Beverley, Jeremy of Caxton and Henry of Bath, Itinerant Justices.

To the Right High and Mighty Prince the Duke of Norfolk, Seneschal of England, shown unto your good and gracious Lordship, the Mair and citizeins of the citee of London. That whereafter the libertee and commendable customs of the said citie of time that no man's mind to the contrary used, enjoyed, and accustomed. The Mair of the said citee for the time being, by reason of the office of Mairaltie of the said citie, in his own person, oweth of right, and duty, to serve the King, our Sovereign Lord, in the day of his ful noble coronation in such place as it shall please his Highness to take his spices; and the same cup, with the keveringe belonging thereto, and a layer of gold, the same Mair to have, and with him to bear away at the time of his departing, for some fee and reward. Also that divers other citizeins, that by the said Mair and city shall be named, and chosen owen of right, by the same custome, at the same day, to serve in the office of Butlership, in the helping of the Chief Butler of England, to the Lords and Estates, that shal be at the said coronation, as well at the table in the hal, at meat, as after meat in the chamber . . . . Also the said Mair and citizeins praien that they may sit, on the day of his said coronation, at the table next the cupboard of the lifte syde of the hal, like as of old time it hath been used and accustomed on the coronation at Westminster, and praying that, *mutatis mutandis*, they might be allowed to exercise the same privilege at the corounation of the queen of Henry VII., July 6, 1501.

Sir John Shaw, Mair.

It was at this time that a dispute arose between the Skinners and the Merchant Taylors[1] respecting their right of precedence in civic processions. The dispute ran high, blows quickly followed, and, as it was a question which did not admit of such a settlement, " the said Maist^{rs}, Wardeyns, and ffeolashipps of both the said p^{r}ties the xth day of Aprill, the first yeere of the Reign of Kyng Richard the iij^{de}, of their free willes have comp^{r}mitted and submitted theymselfs to stonde and obey the Rule and Jugement of Robt Billesdon, Mair, and th' aldremen of the said Citee of London, whereuppon the said Mair and Aldremen takyng uppon theym the Rule, direccion, and charge of Arbitrement of and in the p^{r}misses, ffor norisshing of peas between the Maisters, Wardeyns, and ffeolashipps aforesaid, the which ben ij grete & wirshippful membres of the said Citee, have adjugged and awarded the said Maist^r and Wardeyns of Skynn^{r}s shall yerely desire and pray the said Maist^r and Wardens of Taillo^{r}s to dyne w^t theym atte their Com'on Hall on the Vigill of Corpus Christi; also that the said Maist^r and Wardeyns of Taillo^{r}s shall yeerely desire, and pray the said Maist^r and Wardeyns of Skynn^{r}s to dyne w^t theym on the ffest of the Nativitee of Seint John Bapte, if thei there than kepe an oppen Dyn' at their Com'on Hall, and that the Skynn^{r}s shall goo before the Maist^r, Wardeyns of Taillo^{r}s from the ffest of Easter next comyng unto the ffest of Easter next ensuyng. And that the said Maist^r and Wardeyns shall goo before the Skynn^{r}s after the Feast of Easter next ensuing, and so on alternately, except in the case of the Lord Mair being chosen from one of the Company, in which case the said Company is to have precedency during the yeere."

This judgment of Rich. Billesden has with but one exception

On which occasion the following persons were selected, some of whose names are singularly appropriate to their calling:

    John Tate, Mercer.
    Willm Sands, Grocer.
    Willm Sparke, Cloth^r.
    John Swann, Cissor (*i.e.* Taylor).
    John Ostriche, Haberdasher.
    Willm Mariner, Salter.
    Richd Knight, Fishm^r.
    John Pasmer, Pellipar (*i.e.* Skinner).
    Thos. Breytan, Ironmonger.
    Roger Ford, Vintonner.

[1] Herbert, p. 319; Jor. 6, fo. 105, or No. 9, fo. 50.

during the Commonwealth been faithfully observed; and to this day the Skinners and Merchant Taylors exchange friendly greeting one with another, and take precedence as directed under the award.

The toast used on the meeting of the Companies runs thus:

"The Master, Wardens, and Court of Assistants drink health, happiness, and prosperity to the Master, Wardens, and Court of Assistants of the Merchant Tailors, Merchant Tailors and Skinners, Skinners and Merchant Tailors, root and branch, and may they continue for ever."

The martw as at St. Mary at Axe and St. Andrew Undershaft, a neighbourhood which still retains some of its former local traditions, as any one who cares to visit Leadenhall on its market-days may see.

The charter (16 Richard II.) confirms in perpetuity the Guild of Corpus Christi, by which title the Company of Skinners were then known, and allows them to maintain two chaplains to perform mortuary and other services for brothers and sisters, to appoint a master and four wardens, and empowers them to wear a livery wherein they may make their procession on Corpus Christi.[1] The King also of his special grace, and for lxli. paid into the Hanaper, confirms the former grants of his grandfather's letters patent.

The chantry of Corpus Christi, annexed to St. Mildred Poultry, was established from funds of an earlier endowment in 1394 for a brotherhood, and then took the name of the Chapel of Corpus Christi and St. Mary.[2] When suppressed (1 Edward VI.) its revenue was 10*l*. 8*s*. 8*d*. of which there was allotted to the Skinners' Company yearly two shillings. It did not adjoin St. Mildred's church, but was situated in Conyhope Lane, now Grocers' Hall Court, and the site together with that of a tenement between it and the street is now occupied by the houses Nos. 34 and 35, Poultry.[3]

Subsequent[4] charters were granted by Henry VI. 1430, Henry VII. 1501, Philip and Mary 1558, Elizabeth 1560, and James I. 1606. These charters enter more or less minutely into the trade distinctions

---

[1] See charter of Richard II. This as well as the other charter will be found printed in Herbert's *History of the Twelve City Companies*, p. 308.

[2] The Virgin Mary was the patroness of the Sisters of the Company.—See *Illuminated Court Book*.

[3] Some interesting particulars respecting the chapel and brotherhood will be found in Milbourn's *History of the Church of St. Mildred, Poultry*, p. 20 et seq.

[4] Herbert, p. 308.

of skins dressed and undressed, fell ware and raw ware, empowers the Company to exercise due scrutiny over all articles or men of the same mistery, selling or working in London or elsewhere, or in any fairs, markets, or places throughout England; St. Botolph, Windchester (Winchester), Yves, Stamford, St. Edith, St. Edmonds, and Basingstoke being the principal towns where the trade appears to have settled.

Furs were forbididden under penalty of forfeiture to be worn by any but members of liveries, the royal family, prelates, earls, barons, knights, and ladies, and those in the Church who might expend by the year c livres at the least [1] from their benefices. Coney or rabbit skins were also much worn, both by nobles and gentlemen. The richer furs were of foreign importation, and in early times very costly; mention is frequently made of them in wills as special legacies, but a few examples will suffice.

Joan, Lady Hungerford, bequeaths to the wife of her son Walter her black mantle furred with minever, A.D. 1411.[2]

Joan, Princess of Wales (called also the Fair Maid of Kent), in her will dated in 1385 bequeathed, amongst other things, " Meo carissimo Johanni de Holland (her third son by the Earl of Kent) unum coopertorium de scarlet furr' cum meum purat', 1 couerchief de camaca, sive furrura."[3]

Joan, Lady Bergavenny, 1434, gives her best gown furred with marters (martens) to Walter Kebel; her second gown of marters, and the remnant (remainder) of her gowns so furred, to her son Sir James Osmond.

The most interesting is, however, the will of Dean Colet, 1519, by which he bequeathed to Master (Dr.) Morgan "his best gown, with the hood, his best coat of chamlet furred with black boggys, and a vestment."

Furs were worn both on the gowns and hoods of livery companies. Stowe tells us that the hoods were worn with the roundlets upon the head, the skirts to hang behind the neck. The hoods were in old time made in divers colours according to the gowns, as red and blue, red and purple-murrey, or as it pleased the master and wardens to appoint to their several companies. The gowns were all of one colour, and that, he adds, of the saddest, but the hoods were made of the

---

[1] Statute 11th Edward III. c. 4. This Act was repealed by 1st James I. c. 25.
[2] Herbert, p. 305.   [3] Nichols's *Royal Wills*, p. 79.

same cloth, and the linings remained red, as of old time. The gown is still worn with foins.[1] By the Inspeximus of Elizabeth, 1560, no skinner or furrier was allowed to sell old furs, otherwise than as coming from vestments, that is to say, collars and linings and old hoods with their tippets on.

Furs were packed in tiers, and the number of vents, or bellies as they were called, in each tier is given in the earliest charter (Edward III.); and the same number without any variation is mentioned in those of later date: and other regulations on the same subject were made by the City, as appears by the *Liber Custumarum*, which was compiled about A.D. 1320.[2]

The numbers were as follows:—

Furs of Minever[3]	. . .	8 tiers	120 vents
Do.	do.	7 „	100 „
Do.	Besum	8 „	72 beasts
Do.	Popel[4]	7 „	60 „
Do.	do.	6 „	52 „
Do.	Stradling[5] . . .	6 „	52 „
Do.	Minuta[6] . . .	—	52 „
Do.	Curell	—	60 „
Hoods of Minever, pure	.	—	40 vents
Super fine	do. . . .	—	36 „
Do. do.	. . . . .	4 „	20 „
Do. do.	. . . . .	3 „	8 „

Furs of bogy[7] or boggys, or bennet, or lamb, of one ell or 1¼ in length.

[1] Foins, or foone, fur of the stone marten or fitchet; it is mentioned in the inventory of the wardrobe of King Henry V. taken in 1423, after his decease.—*Prompt. Parvulorum*, and Halliwell's *Dict*, s. v. define it as polecat.

[2] *Liber Albus*, p. 243.

[3] Minever. The furs of the ermine mixed with that of the small weasel. The white stoat is called minefer in Norfolk.—Halliwell's *Glossary*, s. v. Fairholt (*Dict. of Costume*) gives the derivation menu vair, the fur of the black squirrel, which is white beneath. Coleridge (*Glossarial Index*) gives the same derivation.

[4] Pople. The back of the squirrel in spring.—Note to *Liber Albus*, p. 243.

[5] Stranlyng. The skin of the squirrel between Michaelmas and winter.—*Ibid.* note to p. 625.

[6] Minuta—Minuti varii—Menu vairs—Minever.—*Halliwell* and others.

[7] Bogy. Budge fur, *i. e.* lamb-skin with the wool outside. — Halliwell's *Glossary*, s. v.

Beaver (by that name) and various other skins are not mentioned in the earlier charters. All manner of fur which was found contrary to these ordinances was to remain forfeit to the mayor and commonalty of the City, or at the fairs of St. Botolph (Windsor), Winchester, St. Ives, Stamford, St. Edith, and at other fairs in the realm.

One of the duties of the guild also appears to have been to see that all furs were what they purported to be, and that no old ones were sold as new, under pain of forfeiture; this will be seen in the ordinances which we have subsequently noted. Those who worked at the skins were called tauyers, and many disputes used to arise between them and the Skinners. The latter appear to have appointed fairs for furryers, who were formerly associated with Skinners.

By the sumptuary laws passed in the reign of Henry IV.[1] the wearing of furs of ermine, lettice, pure minivers, or grey, by wives of esquires was prohibited, unless they themselves were noble or their husbands warriors or mayors of London. The queen's gentlewomen, attendants upon a princess or duchess, are likewise prohibited from wearing the richer furs.

At a date between 1338 and 1353 the City ordered that common women should not be arrayed in clothing furred with budge or wool. (Letter Book F. 208).[2] And soon afterwards it was ordered that women of evil life should not wear hoods that were furred, except with the wool of lambs or the fur of rabbits. (Letter Book G. 267).[3]

The Corporation guilds formerly joined in royal pageants and processions. When Henry III. (1236) brought home his wife Eleanor, the citizens of London rode out to meet them clothed in long garments embroidered about with gold and silk and divers colours,[4] every man having a golden or silver cup in his hand; again, in the time of Edward I. (1300), when he brought home his wife Margaret from Canterbury, the citizens, to the number of 600, rode out to meet them in one livery of red and white, with the cognizances of their misteries embroidered upon their sleeves. Scarlet gowns and sanguine hoods were worn by the aldermen, and white gowns and scarlet hoods with divers cognizances by the commonalty, in the time of Henry VI. 1432.

[1] Knight's *British Costumes*, p. 180.
[2] *Liber Albus*, p. 510.   [3] *Ibid.*
[4] Stowe, p. 165.

In the time of Henry VII. violet appears to have been worn, the hoods were furred and used as a covering to the head, as may be seen in early missals of that date.

In the charters of Henry VII. (1501) the Skinners are confirmed as to their former privileges under the title of the Master and Wardens of the Guild or Fraternity of the Body of Christ; and the festival of Corpus Christi continues to this day to be especially memorable in connection with the tradition of the guild, when they elect their Master and Wardens for the ensuing year. The ceremony has been often described, but I venture to make some few extracts from the graphic account in Knight's *London*.[1]

"Issuing from their hall in Dowgate in their new liveries they take their places in the procession and pass along the principal street; most imposing is the appearance they present; scattered at intervals along the line are to be seen the lights of more than a hundred waxen torches, costly garnished. Amongst the different bodies included in the procession are some two hundred clerks or priests, in surplices and copes, chanting; after these come the sheriffs' servants, then the clerks of the compters, the sheriffs' chaplains, the Mayor's sergeant, the Common Council, the Mayor and Aldermen in their scarlet robes, and, lastly, the members of the Company, male and female, which it is the business of the day to honour. The church of St. Lawrence in the Poultry is their destination, whither they all proceed to the altar of Corpus Christi and make their offerings, staying awhile to hear mass; from the church they return in the same state to dinner, where the principal and side tables are laid out in all the chief apartments of the building; the officers of the Company occupying one, the sisters another, and the players and minstrels a third. Plate glitters on every side, and choice hangings adorn the hall.

"The materials for the pageant are suspended from the roof, and attract many an admiring glance, while the fragrance of Indian sandal wood is filling the atmosphere, though not altogether to the exclusion of those exhalations which proceed from the kitchen, betokening the more solid pleasure of the epicure.

"The guests, including the Lady Mayoress, with the Sheriffs' ladies, together with Noblemen and the Priors of the great conventual establishments of London, St. Mary Overies, St. Mary Spital, St. Bartholomew, and Christchurch, are all there. Of the dinner itself

[1] *Pictorial History of London*, v. 114.

what shall we say that can adequately describe its variety, profusion, and costliness, or the skill with which it has been prepared ? The boar's heads and the mighty barons of beef seem almost to require an apology for their introduction amidst the delicacies which surround them ; above the stately salt, there are brawn, fat swans, conger, and sea-hog, dishes of great birds, with little ones around them, Lechi Lombard, made of pork pounded in a mortar, with eggs and raisins, sugar, dates, salt, pepper, spices, milk of almonds, and red wine, the whole being tied up in a bladder, with many others of a similar composite character; whilst the subtleties so marvellously and cunningly wrought tell in allegory the history of the company, and of the Saviour as its patron, while it reveals to us the true artist, the cook.

"After dinner, whilst the spiced bread and hippocras goes round, the master and wardens who had retired for election re-enter with garlands on their heads, preceded by the beadle, and the minstrels playing; then the garlands are removed, and a show is made of trying whose head amongst the assistants it will best fit; it is found by a remarkable coincidence that the persons previously chosen by the Court of Assistants are those whom the chaplets do fit.

"With renewed ceremony a loving cup is then brought in, from which the former master and wardens drink health and prosperity to the master and wardens elect, who assume the garlands and are greeted with cheers by the whole fraternity. The pageant is now eagerly looked for, the tables are cleared. The pageant descends from the roof, and the actors, nine in number, approach, and soon the whole audience is engrossed with the representation of the history of Noah's flood."

The coronation of the master and wardens still continues to take place much in the same way at the present time. After the loving cup has gone round a procession is formed by the junior members of the livery in their gowns, bearing caps and silver-gilt cocks, the gift of Sir William Cockain (*see* list of plate), accompanied by the clerk, the beadle with the boys of Christ's Hospital nominated by the Company, preceded by a military band ; twice the hall is perambulated ere the crowns and caps are deposited, when the ceremony of fitting of the cap takes place, amidst a grand flourish of trumpets.

There were also other pageants of processions on Corpus Christi [1]

[1] Stowe, i. 242.

of a very early date, when stage plays were enacted at Clerk's Well, at Skinner's Well, beside Smithfield; they date back as early as 1391, and lasted sometimes three days, and on one occasion we read of Richard the Second and his Queen,[1] with many of the nobility, being present.

It does not, however, appear that there was any miracle-play specially adapted for Corpus Christi day: but rather that the day was selected for the performance of some play based upon Scripture.

A great play is also mentioned by Stowe to have taken place in 1409 at Skinner's Well, which lasted eight days, and was of matter from the creation of the world. The most part of all the great estates of England were there to behold it.[2]

These plays or mysteries, as they were called, were entirely of a sacred character, and similar no doubt to those collected by Mr. J. O. Halliwell-Phillipps, F.S.A., in his work entitled "Ludus Coventriæ," which he says took place on Corpus Christi day, "when a great company of people from far and near assembled to see them acted with mighty state and reverence." The stages were placed high, and generally upon wheels, so that they might be drawn to the principal places for the advantage of the spectators.

In 1450, temp. Henry VII. a tumult was raised against the mayor at a wrestling, beside Clerk's Well.

At Coventry, in 1495, the Cardmakers petitioned that the craft of Skinners and Bakers, who had no play of their own, should pay annually 13s. 4d. towards the charge of their pageants, which the city ordered accordingly. In 1531 the Skinners paid 5s. annually towards the Weavers' pageant.[3]

EARLY COURT BOOKS.

The illuminated court books before mentioned are particularly interesting, both as manuscripts of the fifteenth century and as affording us much important information as regards the customs of the ancient guild.

[1] Stowe, i. p. 251.   [2] *Ibid.* ii. 117.
[3] Sharpe's *Coventry Mysteries*, pp. 10, 11. There were guilds of Corpus Christi at Beverley, founded in 1408, mainly for the performance of such pageants. At Hull and Coventry there were also guilds of Corpus Christi.—Toulmin Smith's *English Guilds*, pp. 141, 154, 160, 232.

The company of corpi xristi
The felawship of oure Lady

Gaudeamus omnes in dño diem festi celebrantes
sub honore bte marie virginis de cuius assumpcõe
gaudent angeli z collaudant filiũ dei·

INSCRIPTION IN HONOUR OF THE VIRGIN ON THE FLY LEAF OF THE COURT BOOK
CONTAINING THE ROLL OF THE COMPANY OF CORPUS CHRISTI AND FELLOWSHIP OF OUR LADY.

The two earliest volumes of records are excellently written upon vellum, and adorned with illuminations: one relates to the Mystery or Craft of the Fraternity of Corpus Christi, being what is now called the Worshipful Company of Skinners; the other is the Roll of the Fraternity of Our Lady. The precise powers and relative position of these two bodies would perhaps be impossible now to ascertain, but their mutual concurrence appears to have been essential to the enactment of the rules and ordinances made from time to time for the good order and governance of either body, all of such rules being specifically stated to be made by the Master and Wardens of Corpus Christi and sixteen of the fraternity of Our Lady.

THE VOLUME RELATING TO THE FRATERNITY OF CORPUS CHRISTI commences with a copy, *in extenso*, of the charter granted by King Richard II., being a confirmation of that granted in the 39th year of King Edward III., A.D. 1365 and 1366. This is succeeded by—

The othe of newe entres and of all shop holders.

Ye shale swere that ye shall be good and trewe liege men unto oure liege lorde the Kyng, and to his heyres kynges; ye shall trewlye by and trewlye sell and trewlye worche after y[e] ordinaunces of the crafte, and as trew workemanship askyth; and all manner ordenaunces lefull and lawfull of this crafte, the secretis and councells of the same, ye shall well and trulic kepe and hold; ye shalbe redy at all manner of Commands that bene made for the worshipe of the Cite and for the Crafte, or ellis to pay youre mercementis that ben ordeyned and assigned therfore; and all the poyntes and ordenaunces longing to the fraunchise of the seid Cite, and for the wele of the seyd Crafte of Skynners, ye shall kepe on your behalue—so god you helpe, and all seyntis.

Then follow the statutes of the Company for the regulation of the trade, commencing thus:—

These bene the Articles touching the Crafte of Skynners of loudon, made by the Good folke of the same Crafte, the whiche bene graunted and confermyd by Adam Burye than mayre of London and the Worshipfull Aldremen of the seid Cite, In the yere of oure soverayne Lorde Kyng Edwarde the thirde, After the Conqueste xxxix[th], (A.D. 1365 & 6) and entred in the book of G., in the leffe, c. lxiij; that is to wytt—

The Articles being of great length, an abstract of them will suffice for the present purpose:—

1. First is ordained that none of the craft work both old and new peltry of his own, so as to avoid suspicion of mixing them.[1]

---

[1] Intermingling new and old work was forbidden in the City at an early date, as appears by the Liber Custumarum (compiled circa 1320).—*Liber Albus*, p. 243.

2. That calabre[1] be used according to its nature, that is to say with one side black, that folk be not deceived.

3. That calabre skins, or gray calabre, of season and not seasoned, be not mixed together nor with popell.

4. Any one proved in the Chamber of the Guildhall to have offended against the above rules, to be imprisoned eight days in Newgate and then fined 13s. 4d. to the Chamber and 11s. 8d. to the Craft, for their Alms.[2]

5. Any man or woman aggrieved by such acts, on complaint to the Rulers of the Craft, to have a good fur instead of that forfeitable, whether put in cloth or not. And, if the offender be a stranger without the City, he shall suffer equally if he can be taken within the franchise.

6. None of the craft to beat fur or skins in the street, under penalty of half a mark, of which half to go to the Chamber and the other half to alms of the craft; and the offender himself to be imprisoned 4 days.[3]

Nor to bring furs of "wilde worke" out of the City till seen by the Rulers to be "avowable," under pain of forfeiture and fine of 5s. to the Chamber and 20d. to alms of the Craft.

Nor to sell furrs of "grey worke"[4] from Flanders or other lands till seen by the Rulers to be true, under like penalties, because the fur of grey brought from Flanders, for the greater gain, is "so stuffed with chalk that unneth[5] a man may not well know them."

7. Any stranger selling ermines, lettues,[6] or work, in the City, making other than good and true "pakking," the same to be sequestrated till he has redressed the fault in the discretion of the craft, or, if a German, then of four of the craft and four of his nation.

8. At accustomed times[7] for the fellowship to wait on the Mayor at "poulis," they go from St. Thomas of Acres to the Bishop's grave in poulis and say *De Profundis*, and there stand in a convenient place in the church, or, if none, in par-

---

[1] Calabre, pelles ex Calabriâ.—*Ducange*.

[2] Furs were forfeited and fines inflicted by the City for mixing old and new work, circa A.D. 1376-99.—(Letter Book H. 39.) *Liber Albus*, p. 521.

[3] The regulations of the City forbid furs to be scoured in the high streets in the day-time, circa A.D. 1309-16.—(Letter Book D. 108.) *Liber Albus*.

[4] Grey work, the back of the squirrel in winter.—*Liber Albus*, p. 243.

[5] Unneth, hardly.

[6] Lettice, a kind of grey fur.—*Halliwell*.

[7] On the morrow of the feast of St. Simon and Jude (if not a Sunday) the new mayor went to St. Thomas de Acon, and thence with the Aldermen to St. Paul's, where, at a spot in the middle of the nave, between the two small doors, it was the custom to pray for the soul of Bishop William, who, it is said, procured from King William the Conqueror great liberties for the City of London; thence to the tomb of the parents of St. Thomas of Canterbury in the churchyard, and back to St. Thomas of Acons, where the Mayor and Aldermen each offered a penny.—*Liber Albus*, p. 24. Stow says, Thomas of Acons was situated on the north side of Cheap Street, at ye Great Condnit. Vol. i. p. 37.

done church halle,[1] in order, till the Mayor has passed, under penalty of 8d., half to the Chamber and half to the alms.

9. On 22nd June, in the 28th year of King Henry VI. (1449), the Master and Wardens, and 16 of the most wise and discreet of the Fellowship of Skinners, unanimously agreed that if any suitable member of the fellowship or of the Brotherhood of Corpus Christi, being duly elected to be Master or Warden, refuse to serve, he be fined 10 li. without favour or pardon.

10. On the same day it was ordained that any Brother of Our Lady's Fellowship elected to the aforesaid Office and refusing to serve be fined 5 li.

11. On 2nd June in the 1st year of King Edward IV. (1461), it was enacted by the like authority, that any of the Craft when warned by the Bedell and not attending in the Hall at 7 o'clock, or other hour set, shall pay 8d. to a pound of wax; the master or wardens double. Failing to be present before the stroke of 9, to be fined 8d. without redemption.

On 6th January in the 3rd year of King Edward IV. (1462-3), it was ordained by like authority, that the Fellowship of the Skinners in the Clothing of the Brotherhood of Corpus Christi be warned by the beadle and attend in their livery with the Master and Wardens at St. Thomas of Acres on Christmas Day, the Wednesday following New Year's Day, the Twelfth Day, and Candlemas Day, to bring the Mayor to St. Paul's, under fine of 12d. to the box of Corpus Christi; and that none pretend (unduly) to be wardens, under penalty of 3s. 4d.

12. On 11th January in the 17th year of King Edward IV. (1476-7), it was ordained by like authority, that any freeman of the craft making suit, of evil will, to any other fellowship to change his copy, whether covertly or openly, shall pay c mares sterling, one half to the Chamberlain of London towards the common coffers of the City, and the other half to the sustentation of the poor men of the Craft.

13. On 24th Feb. in the 2nd year of King Henry VII. (1486), it was enacted by the Master and Wardens of the Skinners, with the assent of the 16 of the Fellowship of Corpus Christi, that one who has been Master shall have in seven years four apprentices, Wardens three, and others two.

14. None to take an apprentice till personally approved by the Master, and proved to be free-born and not lame or disfigured of limbs, whereby the City nor Craft take disworship in time coming; and also pay a fee of 20s. to the Wardens: under penalty of 26s. 8d. without redemption. The Clerk of the Company of Corpus Christi to engross the Indentures and enter them in the Register.

15. None to take an apprentice unless of "abilitie of connyng" to teach him the Craft, and keep and find him. If default be found by the Master and Wardens they to remove the apprentice to another master.

16. "The othe of the newe maister and wardeyns the morowe after the day of corporis xpi.

"Ye shall swere that ye shalbe true liegemen unto oure liege lorde the Kyng, and to his heyres Kyngs; ye shall be indifferent Jugis betwene party and party, withoute favoure, love, or affeccion, and withoute malice or any evill will to

---

[1] Pardon-Church-Haugh, part of St. Paul's churchyard, on the north side, eastward of the Bishop's palace.—Dugdale's *St. Paul's*, p. 93.

any parsone or parsons, All manner ordenaunnces and good rules that bene made or shall be made for the wele of this craft of Skynners, ye shall truly execute and kepe; ye shall not bruke any of the ordenaunces made by þe comyn Assente and hole agrement of all the xvi of thys Companye w'onte þe hoole agrement of alle (or of þe most part, interlined) þe same xvi. All these thyngs ye shall truly observe and kepe; so helpe you god and all seynts, and by the boke; & kys hyt, &c."

17. On 14th July, in the 17th year of King Edward IIII. (1477), it was ordained by like authority that any man's son if apprenticed to himself pay no fee.

18. On 3rd October, in the same year, it was ordained that none take any man's servant or apprentice to lodge or work in his house without leave of the wardens or master under penalty of 40s.

19. Whereas at divers times the master and wardens have in certain years bought themselves livery of the finest cloth, to the great cost of the common box of the fellowship, it is now ordained and enacted that they shall not take, in the years of giving of livery, more than other years, viz., 20d. and no more.

20. On 6th Jan., the 19th year of King Edward IIII. (1478-9), it was ordained that no Skinner shall make complaint of another in the Counter, or Mayor's Court, without leave of the master or wardens; and in default to pay for each offence to the alms 6s. 8d., without remission or favour.

21. On the 24th Jan., the 6th year of King Henry VII. (1490) it was ordained by William Martyn, Alderman, the master, and the wardens and the 16, that the master and wardens grant no lease of lands, rents, or tenements, for more than a year, without consent of the 16, under penalty, if done by the master or wardens, of 10l. to the alms, without redemption.

MEM.—21st May, the 9th year of King Henry VII. (1493), it is ordained by Wm. Martyn, Mayor, and the Aldermen, and recorded in the books of the City in the Guildhall of London, that no stranger or foreigner take upon himself the occupation of the craft of Skinners under penalty of 6s. 8d., half to the Chamberlain of London and half to the fellowship.

Also, that none of the fellowship hereafter employ any journeyman, except a freeman; upon proof and certificate to the Chamberlain of London to forfeit every time 20s., half to Chamberlain, and half to the fellowship; Thomas Goldherst then being Mayor.

The names of the Founders and Bretheren and Sisters of the fraternity of Corpus Christi founded by the Worshipful Fellowship of Skynners of the Citie of London, that is to say:

King Edward the III.	King Henry the V.
Dame Philip his Queen.	Dame Kat'ryn his Queen.
Kyng Richard the II.	Kyng Henr' the VI.
Dame Anne his Queen.	Kyng Edward the IIII.
Prince Edward, father of the said King Richard.	Dame Elizabeth his Q^e.
	Leonell Duke of Clarence.
King Henry IIII.	Henr' Duke of Lancastre.
Dame Johan his Queen.	Thomas Duke of Clarence.

John Duke of Bedford.
Humphrey Duke of Gloucess'.
Richard Duke of York.
John Duke of Excestre.
George Duke of Clarence.
Richard Duke of Gloucess'.
Edmund Erle of Rutland.
Richard Erle of Salesbury.
John Lord ffaunhope.
Sir John Levirton, clerk.
Sir Water Edynh'm, clerk.
Sir Water Sasseley, clerk.
Sir Thomas Pattishull, cl'.
Sir Thos. Blunell, clerk.
Sir Robert Ellerker, clerk.
Sir Thomas
Sir John Brampton, cl'.

Sir John Cambrigge, phesician.
Davy Lecke.
Nicholas Longe, clerk.
Frere Water Brig'.
Sir John Everdon.
Sir Thomas Solding, clerk.
Water Brikkilliswade.
Sir James Walker, p'son of Seynt John's walb°ke.
John Newport.
Sir John Spark, clerk.
John Bedford, wulman.
Pers of Newcastel.
Master Nychol Barshal, prest of corpus xp'i.
and others to the number of 592.

Then follow the names of the Sisters:
> Dominica soror testamenta, including,
>> My lady Alys Dulgrene.
>> My lady dam Ali' Bryce.
>> My ladi dā ysbell Norburght.
>> My lady Jone Adderley.
>> Marg'et Croke.
>> Alys Goldwyn.
>> My lady dam Mgt Alley.
>> Margarete viscounte' Lesse.

and others, in all 111.

Then follow a list headed with four aldermen and 204 others, which, together with the entrance of new brethren at the feast of Corpus Xpi. a°. do^i. M.CCCC. IIIJ^{xx}. XVIIJ., and in the succeeding years 10, make altogether about 720 of the fraternity, which is closed with the name of Harry Wilkyns, clerk of the craft.[1]

[1] H.R.H. Henry Frederick Augustus Duke of Cumberland and Strathern, Earl of Dublin, one of His Majesty's Most Honourable Privy Council, was admitted to the freedom in 1767, together with the Right Honourable Charles Townsend. The late Lord Strangford, a lineal descendant of Sir Andrew Judd, and Lord Clyde, were also members. On the 19th of July, 1673, the Right Honourable Lieutenant Berkley of Berkley, and Lord Mowbrey Hargrave of Prussia, were added to this list of freemen.

Another extract gives the connection of the guild with other towns where their influence extended. I select this because it shows that other trades were also admitted to the fellowship:—

These be the names of the brethen and sistren in ye tyme of John Wynter, John Aūger, Richard Scarlet, Thomas mace, Wardeyns of ye seid fraternyte of oure lady,[1] ye xxv day of Julii ye xxiiij ȝere of king Harry ye sixte. (1445).

    Marster john boner, doctour.
    John moūfort, gentilmā, of reigate.
    Pers carpenter, of reigate.
    John melelard, of reigate.
    John wodeward, bocher.
    John wrixwope, gentilman.
    John huntūgdon, of seint albons.
    John higdon, dier.
    John thorpe wadisbiry, gentilmā.
    William at þe wode, of bristowe isoperey.
    Willam haselingfeeld, joyner.
    John white, of charlewode.
    John peinter, of salisbury, skynner.
    John gold, bocher.
    John petite, groser.
    Thos. Winkborne of aldenham.
    Harry camproun.
    Isabel molling, silkwijf.
    Richd. pleistowe.
    John aischlee, of godstoone.

A lawe made bytwene the landlord and the tenaunt.

In the tyme of Cateworthe Mayre of London, the xxiij yere of the reign of Kyng Henry the sixt, the olde books recordes processes and jugementes serched and sene. It was declared by the same Maire and Aldermen than beyng, that it shall not be liefull to eny tenaunt for terme of life, or for terme of yeres, within the said Citee at the ende of his terme, or at eny other tyme, to cast downe, take awey, or pull up eny easment to the houses in the grounde of his seid tenure by hym nayled or fastned either with naile of yren, or of tymber as a pentyce, a staple for a lok, glass latyce, a benche, or other like, nor eny aisement fastned with morter, whether the same morter be of lyme or of cley, as a ffurneys, an oven, a chymney, a pavement, and such other, nor any plante, or tree, sett in the grounde, that hath taken roote as vynes, trees, busshes, and suche other.

---
[1] St. Thomas of Acres, Spital, and Bethlehem.

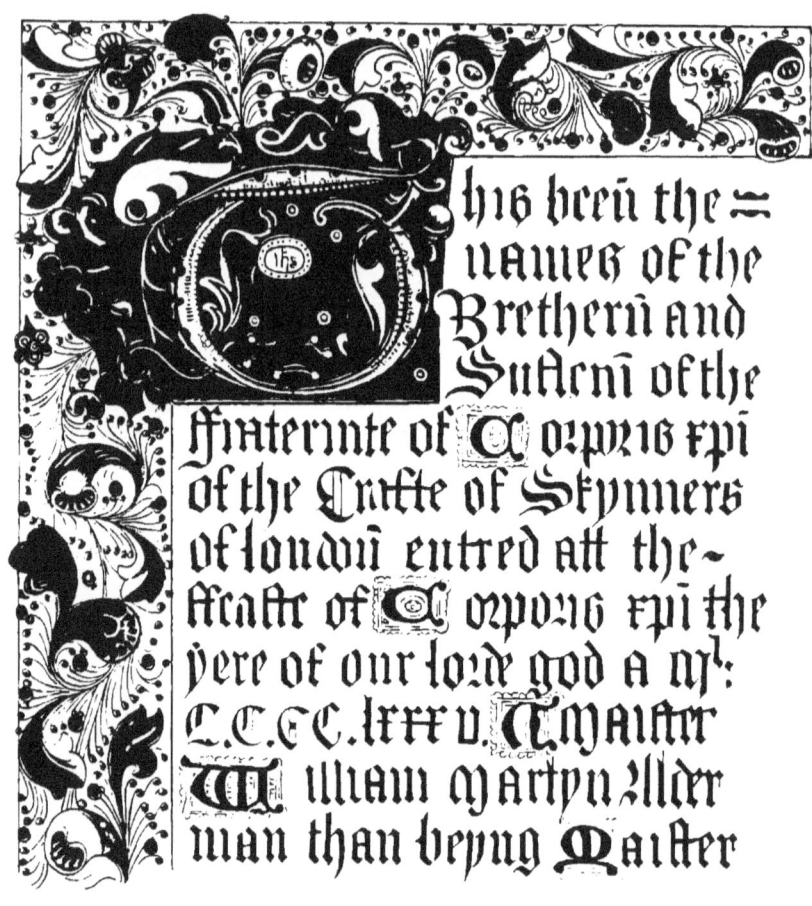

·: Illumination from the Books of the Skinners Company :·

After these articles are entered year by year the names of the master and wardens, each year in a separate column, headed with the chalice and host, indicative of the guild of Corpus Christi, and with other rich illuminations in colours. The usual heading ran thus till 1548 :—

> These been the names of the Bretheren and Systeren of the ffraternity of Corpus Xpi of the Crafte of Skynners of London, entered att the ffeast of Corpus Xpi the yeare of our lorde god M^{l}ccccclxxxv. Maister William Martyn, Alderman, than being Maister of the seide ffraternite and crafte; Richard Swan, Olyu' Caston, Thomas Busseleon and Roger Swanloft, than being Wardyns.

After this date it was customary to enter the heading thus :—

> These be the names of the master and the wardens of the ffelawshypp of Corpus Christi of the Skynners of London, entered at the fest of Corpus Xpi in the yere of ower lorde M^{l}cccccxlviij.

The illumination of the chalice and host, accompanied by the monograms IHS and XPS, contained in the initial of each year's entry, appears for the last time in the year 1579, after which date it was superseded by a royal crown—a good emblem of the supersession of the church by the State.

From the year 1550 the arms of the Company head each page, the helmet being that of an esquire and closed until 1612, after which it was represented as open.

It is noteworthy that the entries are always stated to be made on the feast of Corpus Christi, even through the whole period of Puritan rule : and the royal crown, surmounted by its lion, and with the Prince of Wales' plume boldly illuminated, were never intermitted ; this speaks strongly for the determined religious loyalty of the Company.

In the latter portion of the book the arms of England and Scotland are introduced, together with the arms of the Russia and Muscovy merchants, as well as those of Ebbing and Eastland, and merchants of the Levant.

Occasionally we meet with the name of a clerk of the Company, such as Henry Wilkins, Corporis Xpi. 1504, Master John Batten, A.D. 1556, and Thomas Pennant, 1639. In the 19th of Edward IV. we find the following entry relating to the " clerks wagy^s " :—

> Item it is ordeyned in this same yere be the Master and Wardennys, and the xvi of Corpus Xp'i, and the xvi of our ladies ffelisschyp, that Thomas Mason

that tyme beyng clerk of the said felyschypp shall have yearly fro this day for his salary xl s.

The name of Master William Jenyns, Dean of Gloucester, appears as a member of the Guild in 1544.

The volume relating to the fraternity of Our Lady commences with a series of rules for the governance of that body, which throw much light upon its organisation, and, being otherwise curious, are given in extenso, as follows:—

Memorandū that it ys ordeynyd and assēted be the maisterys and wardennys of the crafte of skynneris with the xvj off ye company of Corp'is xpi. And be the wardennys and ye xvi of the bretheryn and ffelawship of oure lady. The xxiiij day of April In the yeer of oure lord god m.iiij^{c}lxxij. And the xii yeer of kyng Edward the iiijth. That euery brodir of oure lady felyschip beyng skynn' holdyng ony schoppe or chambyr of the same That he schall yeerly take an hoode clothe of the wardennys for the yeer beyng or ellys that yeer that no leuery ys gewȳ that he schall pay for the incresse of the clothe xx^d. And that he schall come with his hoode redy made uppon his schulder on oure lady day Assumptōn to scyute Thomas of Acrysse and awayte uppō the wardennys of o^r lady ffelawship so comyng forth unto the churche of seynt John uppon Walbroke. And there to offer at the hyee Masse or ellys to pay for the defaunte to the Box of our Lady iij. s. iiij^d. w^{t}oute ony redempcōn. Also it is ordeynyd that iiij p'sonys skynn's of the xvj. of oure lady bretherhode schalbe schosyn to see and understōde that the clothe that schalbe bowgth and ordeyned for the levery schalbe yn valure of iii.s. iiij d. the yarde.

Also we provide and ordeyne that ev'y broder of the felyschip beyng assigned schall come at ony tyme that he is warned he the Clerk for ony obit of broder or sistir dissessed with his levery hoode that he is warned to come yn uppon the peyne of 1 pounde wax. Also we ordeyne and assent that euery brodir off the same ffelischyp schall come to the dyner as he is Warned. And if he come not he schall pay nev' the lesse. And iff ony brodyr be syke or dissesyd and may not come and so knowyn y^t he may send to the skynnys halle to the wardennys for the yeer beynge ffor his dyn', viij.d. so that he come be fore the fyrst corsse be servydyn. That thanne he schall haue for his porcōn as schall for oon man be hit hoo snevyr hit he of the seyde bretheryn or systeryn.

Also eve'ch of the seide[1] ffrat'nite thats taken[2] clobinge ne shal not[3] de foyll ne mysuse her clothinge ne[4] done it away withjnne two yere in poyne to paye to the almesse of ye seid frat'nite iij s. iiij d. but wel and honestly kepe it and[5] were it in worship of all ye same frat'nite, and that every brother at the[6] receyvynge of the clothinge paye he fore iij s. iiij d. and the[7] remennte as the Wardeynes & he may accorde.

[1] fraternity.
[2] clothing.
[3] defyle nor misuse their clothing.
[4] nor do away with it.
[5] wear it.
[6] receiving.
[7] rest.

THE COMPANY OF SKINNERS. 21

Also yif eny of the same frat'nite be chosen for to be[1] broÞ'e [2] of ye maisters of the Craft of Skynners he he shal not take no cloÞinge of the[3] .... for the tyme that he taketh clothinge of the maisters[4] nev'ye lees he shal be take for oon of ye bretherhode yif he do his duetees as a broÞ' doth.

Also yer bene accorded that ye same ffrat'nite shall fynde v tapers of[5] Wexe on the beem[6] in the Chapel in the church of seint John[7] up Walbrok above seid in Worship of the V Woundes that his blessed body suffred on ye cros for the redemption of al man kynde to[8] brenne ev'y solempne daye at divine s'vice, And also eu'ech brother or sistre that dyen shullen have at her[9] entierments six new torches,& two tapers of Wexe, eech taper of xx lb brennynge at her [10] dirigees and at masses of Requiem as longe as this fraternite lasteth. And also yif there be eny Wif of eny broÞ'e that dye after Þat the brothere her husbond hath [11] be in ye forseid bretherhede by vii yere fulli she shal have the light hool as thoo she were a sust'r of the same co'pany yif she wil axe it.

Also yif eny of ye same ffrat'nite dye eve'ch of the same frat'nite there shollen be at her [12] entierment the which shal be done ye sononday next folowinge and ye body dede shal have foure masses & eve'ch offre aftere his devocion & ye body to be borne to the place there he shal be buried, And ther dwelle til the Corps be assoyled, And who so faile of hem shal paye for ev'ech defaulte that he fayleth iiij d. But if he may excuse hȳ be excusacions afterward writen. And more over yif eny of ye seide frat'nite dye out of Town as in pilg'mage or sodeyne deth, Þat god forbede, and have no frendship to make there entierment the Wardaynes for Þe yere shollen do it uppon ye frat'nite cost. fery' more if eny of the seide ffrat'nite dye eny sodeyn deth as be theves or watere, that god forbede, with inne vij myle aboute ye Cite of london above seid, all the bretheren of the same frat'nite there sholl be hym to bringe to the Citee aboven seid Þif ther mowe be ony waye have leve.[13]

---

[1] brotherhood.
[2] The letter y, as in this instance, is occasionally written in this document instead of the semi-Saxon Þ.
[3] word erased.
[4] nevertheless.
[5] wax.
[6] candle-beam, or rood-loft.
[7] upon.
[8] burn.
[9] interment.
[10] Dirige.
[11] been in.
[12] interment.
[13] Stowe, p. 259, mentions the following circumstance in connection with this rule: Thomas Percey, anno 1561, late Skinner to Queen Mary, was attended to his burial in St. Mary Aldermary Church with twenty black gowns and coats, twenty clerks singing, twelve mantle frieze gowns worn by as many poor men; rails set up in the church where the corpse was to rest, hanged with black and arms. Three dozen of escutcheons of arms, and the floor strewed with rushes. For the chief mourners, Mr. Crowley preached. There were present all the cloathing of the Mystery of Skinners, afterwards a great dole of money, and then all went home to dinner. The Company of Skinners to their hall to dine together. At this funeral all the mourners offered, so did the said Company. In Walbroke Church there is a monument to the memory of Daniel Brown, who was Skinner to all kings and queens of the realm from the year 1660 to 1698.

Also yif eny of the same frat'nite trespas to other to him þat the ts'pas is shal be made shewinge of his harmes and greefes to the Wardeyns and the Wisest of ye same frat'nite and ther shollen so redresse it and be accorden and the trespasour make to ye partie agreved resonable amendis and pay over that to the ffrat'nites almesse ii lb. wex in her g'ce. And in every manere is ordeyned of hem yat bene, hauen bene, and shollen bene misdoinge or misspekynge to eny of her bretheren of ye forseide frat'nite, and wil not obeye hym to amendent be aware of the same frat'nite he shall be putt ont of þe same frat'nite til he have made amendys for þe trespas done to ye said frat'nite.

Also alle the bretheren of þe same frat'nite have bene by v'rtue of ye charter to the craft of Skynners be our worthie excellent and noble kynge Ric'd the second above seid ys g'nnted to assemblen togider certeyn tymes in þe yere yif it be for profite of the same frat'nite as oft hem best liketh and shollen be thereof warned. And yif eny be absent yei shollen pay for ev'y defante iiij d. but if he may excuse him be siknesse or lettinge of eny Ryal [1] of ye rewme or of his maister or ont of contre or eny other resonable cause.

Also yif eny of ye same frat'nite falle in poverte by eny myschief or siknesse or by eny ōr way and hath bene vij yere dwellinge in þe forseid frat'nite and paide and p'formed alle þe poyntes and ductees aft' his power to þe forseid frat'nite [2] longinge withjnne the forseide tyme than he shal have of þe almesse of the frat'nite be deliverannce of þe Wardeynes [3] þerof xiiij d. eve'y weke and an hode of lyvere of the same frat'nite every yere duringe his poverte.

Also yif eny of the same frat'nite be [4] enp'soned falsly be envie, or be fals

---

At Norwich was the guild of the Peltyors (under the patronage, not of Corpus Christi, but of Holy Trinity), founded in 1376, the rules of which were generally similar.—*Ibid*. p. 28.

Similar entries are also fonnd in Machyn's Diary, who was himself a member of the Merchant Taylors' Company:—

P. 233. 1560. The xxx day of Aprell was bered in sant Gregore chyrche in Powlles chyrche-yerd master Payne skynner, and gayff armes, and ther was the masturs of compene of the Skynners in ther (livery,) he had a sermon.

P. 255. 1561. The sam day was bered in Cornyll mastores Hunt wedow, and the chylderyn of the hopetall and the masters wher at her berchyng with ther gren stayffes, and the xxx chylderyn syngyng the Pater-noster in Englys, and a xl pore women in gownes; and after the clarkes syngyng, and after the corse, and then mornars, and after the craftes of the worshephull compene of the Skynners; and ther dyd pryche the byshope of Durram master Pylkyngtun; and after to the Skynners halle to dener.

P. 176. 1558. The xij day of October was bered in Althermare parryche Raff Prestnu, skynner, &c. . . . and the masters of the cloythyng of the Skynners was ther; and after they whent to the Skynners' hall to dener.

P. 224. 1560. The xxx day of January was bered in sant Margettes-moyses master Busse skynner, on of the masturs of the hospetall, and ther was all the masturs of the hospetall with gren stayffes in ther handes, and all the masters of ys compene.

[1] royal person.
[2] belonging.
[3] thereof.
[4] imprisoned

THE COMPANY OF SKINNERS. 23

hatrede take, wherfor he may not maintene him silf to lyve and dwelled in ye manere aforeseid he vij yere in the same frat'nite and paide and p'formed alle ye poyntis and ductees aft' his power withjnne ye forseid tyme yan he shal have xiiij d. ev'y weke duringe his meschief be delyu'ance of the wardeynes.

Also for as moch as all ye same frat'nite shol not be letted ev'ich tyme þat ony nede is in ye forseid frat'nite no assemblen all hoole be togidere,[1] but if it were for the grettere nede howe so eve' ye wardeyns for þe yere done forth with xij other associed to hē alle the hole frat'nite shullen holden hem agreed þerwith, as wel for clothinge as for alle other thinges of charge longing to the same companye. And which of þe xij warned to come to eny nede and come not, but he may excuse hȳ be resonable excusations shal paye at eny tyme that he failleth iij s. iiij d.

Also for as miche as the goodys of þe same frat'nite have bene betyme passed be defaute of hem þat han bene kepers [2] p'of to grete [3] aventersynge of alle the companye almes myskeped and mysrewled, ordeyned is and assented that whan ye wardeyns for the yere passed shullen chese the wardeyns for þe yere sewinge þei shol be bovnden for þe same men that þei chosen in such a co'dition that if it so be falle as god forbede þat the goodes of the seide frat'nite be hindred, harmed, or [4] liteled, in her tyme that ben chosen for the yere new it shal be re'd[5] of hem that chesen such wardeynes, as wel as of hem þat þe faute is founden jnne, so that the goodes of þe same frat'nite shollen no more be litteled as it hath bene.

Also ye wardeynes of þe same frat'nite shollen ev'y yere [6] yelden her rekekenynge (sic) to an xx of the best of alle the same frat'nite of all receites and expenses made in þe vse of the cōpanye also, and of [7] enqeete of cloþing for ye yere passed be Wadenesday in ye Estre weke next suynge, the feest ev'y yere of Corpus X¹ at þᵉ feryest, wiþont eny more puttinge ove' jn þem ev'ech of ye wardeyns þᵗ bene for the tyme to paye to yᵉ cōpany almesse vj s. viij d.

Also þei bene accorded that ev'y yere on our lady day the Assūpcion all the bretbered shullen assemble [8] hool to gider in þe chirch of seint John up Walbroke above seide, ther to here an hie masse in þe worship of þe p'cions sacramēt of the [9] autre v'r°y god is owne body ev'eth to offre after his devocion'is. And which of al this forseid bretherhede faile shal paie to þe cōpanye almesse iiij d., but if he may excuse him be excusations a fore rehersed.

Also assented is and accorded þat the same fraternite shullen every yere holden a feest or a diner to [10] gidere if it be likinge unto hem þe which shal be made the day of the feest of the Assūpcion of our lady above seid, þif it be day of flessh and þif it be not ye sononday next followinge. And which of þe same frat'nite, and he be of power þat absent him, but if it be [12] be v'rey trewe excusation shal paye as moche as yough he were yere.

---

[1] all the whole, together.	[2] thereof.
[3] adventuring—risk.	[4] lessened.
[5] ? required; word scarcely legible.	[6] produce or yield.
[7] enquiry.	[8] altogether.
[9] altar.	[10] together.
[11] to considere.	[12] by.

Also all the bretheren and sustrē of this forseid frat'nite that were in the frat'nitees of seint mary spitell, and of bethleem, whoos vij yeres of ye gretter quarterages þat is forto witte xvj d. be yere bene wered out and passed shollen stonde forth stille in this forseid fraternite as þei did in that other. And so alle oþer¹ of ye same wiþjnne yoos seuen yeris stondinge forth stille after þe quantite of her yeres for disturbance of payment of quart'ages.

Also for as mochel as ye wardeines of this forseid bretherod þat shollen bere the t'vaille for alle ye company shold falle be alle reson and exp'ience due worship as falleth be bretheredes to be so' perfor ordeynd is and assented þᵗ what manere brother of þe same bretherede yþat² mishave him in eny manere þinge, in worde or in dede, that sholde tñ'e vilenye or repreef to eny of the same wardeynes be ye tyme that thei dwelle in her office that may be ³ preued be foure good men and trewe, the trespasour shal make amendis at ev'y tyme that he t'spaseth iiij lb. wexe. And also þif ye wardeynes for þe tyme because that thei shold ⁴ norssh love most amonge the bretherede, mishave hē or mishere hē as is aboñ seide þᵗ may also be p'ved be four trewe men þei sholl renne in ye double peyne.

Also for as mich as he that hath be be⁵ litel tyme knower of a companye sholde not be reson governe a companye as he þat hath knowen a cōpanye of longe time, and fauty of gov'nō'ce be waye of unkōuynge maye gretly distrouble a companye' ordeyned is and assented þat what maner man shal bere ye office of wardeynship in this same cōpanye, the tweyn at leest shollen be such as haven dwelled in þe same bretherod vij yere at þe leest. And þe other tweyn that have dwelled in þe same companye four yere at þe leste, no⁶ þinge doynge in her office, as in ⁷ byinge and ⁸ prisinge of clothinge newe men into the same companye receivynge almesse to eny pore brother or sustre, g'nntinge light to eny brother, sustre, or brotheris wif, grauntinge or over sight of dynere and alle oþer charges ov' seynge upon peyne eche of þe wardeynes to paye at ev'y time that thei faile in this iij s. iiij d. to the almesse of the same companye.

And for ease of þe same wardeyns also and in drawinge forth of men þat bene ripe and have borne none office in þe same Companye' ordeyned is and assented that who so bereth þe charge of Maistership shall not occupie that office be v yere after that he hath borne charge thereof.

Also the xxxiij day of Fev'yere the yere of þe regne of kinge Henr' ye fourte ye thred, ordeyned is assented and fulli ⁹ g'unted to be holden kept first be ye maister of the craft William Framchingh'm than shyriff of london, and be his waydeyns, that is to witte, Thos. Rolf, John Pellynge, John Hows, and Richard Ffrekell, and afterwardes be ye wardeyns for ye same yere of ye ¹⁰ yemen companye þat is to witte, Richard Redinge, Thos. Ledrede, William Sotton, and john morpath, and ¹¹ fery'more be all ye wisest of þe same companye that þe companye is

¹ other. ² misbehave in any manner or thing.
³ proved. ⁴ promote.
⁵ been by. ⁶ nothing.
⁷ buying and. ⁸ pricing.
⁹ granted. ¹⁰ yomen?
¹¹ furthermore.

ordeyned to be rewled by. That for as myche as ther bene mony of þe same Companye þat paien to evel[1] her quarteraiges and for cloth, and other maner ductes that be longeth to the companye, that þei þat paien wel and trewly bene gretly vilanyed and agreved, and ye almesse may nnnethis be mayntened and fery, more þe companye stonte in poynt to be undo, yat God forbede, for evil wille and hevynesse that thei þat done wel and trewly her ductees beren to ye company be cause of þe evel name yat the evel parers make þe companye to have and to bere. And also every yere þe wardeynes as all ye cōpanye knowen wel haven mony sore t'vailles aboute the Tovne fro þe begynnynge of þe yere to þe endinge, that it is [2] vilcinye to alle þe copanye yat so litel þinge is so longe to paye not withstondinge every yere ye Wardeynes gret t'vaile and her losse of her good, ordeyned is and assented be the maister above seid and the wardeyns and be all ye wisest of the companye that there shal no brother nor sustere of þe same company here no newe cloþinge of the companye lyve,[4] no newe yere nor be take to comune amonge his bretheren as a brother shold be into þe tyme þat he have ful paide and made a ful ende of alle maner dettys and ductees þ[t] he oweth to the companye and to þe wardeynes of þe yere laste before passed as touchinge for eny [3] maner þinge þt[4] longeþ to the brotherhede uppon peyne of ye newe wardeynes ever her after that if þei deliver eny such old detto, eny uewe cloþinge more or lasse til be haue paide the Wardeynes last before hē þat he oweth to hem, as for clothinge and to ye cōpany al þat he oweth of dettys to ye companye thei þat deliver hem eny [5] þinge of newe shal paye both to the Wardeynes last before hem and eke to all ye cōpanye all þat þei owen olde.

Also ye xxiij daye of ffev'yere ye xiij yere of þe reiyne of kinge Henrye þe vi[th] ordeyned and assented is, and fulli g'unted to be holden and kept ffirst be the assent and ye a'vice of ye sextene, and in þe tyme of Thos. Coly, Ric. Burdon, John Grene, and John Poule, þt tyme Wardeynes of þe frat'nite for the yere shal hold a [6] diryge att Seint Job'is in Walbroke þe sat'day afore þe daye of her dyner, and whan þe dirige is done, to have þo[r] drinkinge at þe halle for alle ye saules of alle þe bretheren and þe sustren to fore past paying to ev'y prest and to ev'y clerk of þe said Seint John is Chirch iiij d. and on ye morowe eft' at ye masse of requiem, and so go to mete and to the which ordinauce ye scid maisters wy the afore seide han fully awarded that what Wardeyns that this dirige and ye masse unholden and unserved shall paie to þe same frat'nite to the helpinge of her almesse v li. of money wyout eny redempcion.

The rules are followed by a list of "names of the old bretheren holden at Seint Mary-Spitel and at Bethleem the which continues forth a yess [7] brethren in the newe."

The next list is headed: "These bene the bretheren and the susteren that entered inne after þe makyng of þe black paupers." Then follow

[1] pay too evilly, make default in payment.
[2] villany.   [3] manner of thing.
[4] belongeth.   [5] thing.
[6] dirge.   [7] thenceforth?

various entries, of which the following are selected as being those of most general interest:—

There is delivered be the hondes of þe seid Richard Bridford, John Gilmyn, Andrew Sutton, and Richard Maldon, unto Richard Honyngton, Tho⁸ Sheerd, William Wikwane, and Gybon prest þe x day of Juyl in the yere of king henry ye v^{te} þe viij yere a dosen sponys of silver þe which weien xiiij unc' and a qt'on p'ce þe unc' ij s. vj d. without the makinge The whiche margerie Redinge hath yeu'e unto þe bretheren and the sustren of þe same companye in that entent forto s've at the sustres table at her dinere in mynde of hir. þe some xxxv s. vij d.

Also be it remembred that at ye accounte of ye seid Wardeines at her deliv'ance up of the boxe they laft ther Inne in money liiij l. viij s. viij d.

Next is an interesting inventory of the goods of the fraternity made on the 18th July in the 20th year of King Henry VI. (1441).

These bene the goodes the whiche remayne to the bretheren of the seid frat'nite in the tyme of the seid wardeyns at her acounte. Wiþ money Jnells and ornamentȝ.

First in money in the box   iiij^{xx} li. xiij s. v d.

Also a Chales with a caas therto weyinge xv unc. & an half and a q'rto'n.

Also a maser p'ce xl s. of ye gift of Thomas ffrankssc whose name is writen in the bordure of ye bone of the same cup.

Also a nother maser p'c.   x s.

Also ij masbokes A chesible of cloth of gold with crovnes of Estrich fetheres. with avbe. sto!e. amyte. ffanon. & girdell.

Also a nother Chesible of ȝalowe ȝarcsenet. with avbe. amyte. stole. fanon. and girdell. with a fruntel of ye same.

Also a chesible of rede saten with the apparaille.

Also a Chesible of white silk with the apparaill.

Also a pleyn towale with a fruntell for an anter of Rede and blewe tarteryn for un avtere.

Also an avter cloth of blak tarteryn beten with Estrich fetheres, and lynes.

Also an avtercloth of grene tarteryn beten with palys.

Item a fruntel for an awter of white with Roses.

Also a bordcloth drapred holdinge vj ȝerdes. A bordcloth of drapre holding iij ȝerdes. A Touale drapred cōteynynge xiij ȝerdes (and an half—struck out.)

Also ij bordeclothes pleyn conteyninge xxx yerdes.

Also the seid wardeynes han ordeyned and do make this regestr' boke in p'cell of her entres, the valewre to   xxx s.

Almost every year records some donation such as those in the following examples:—

Remembrance that Agnes the wiff of John Raye Skynner hath yiven to god and in the worship of his blessed moder in whos name this Bretherhede is founded to the use of the seide frat'nite of y^s seide yere xl. s. And William Brembyll pynner undere the seid forme vjs viij d.

Also the seide Wardeyns han yevē in parcell of ther encrece in this seide yere vj newe torches weying vj^xv and viij lb. Of the which ther was of olde wex lviij lb. p'ce the lb. iiij. d. And so byleveth in clere of newe wex at viij d. the lb.

iij li. vjs.

Also Alys ffranke hath yeven to ye seid fraternite in this yere a towel conteynyng v yerdes qrt' of diapre werk.

Also the seide Wardeynes have yeven up at their Acounte in the seide yere abouen ye some receyved at her incomyng of clere money as it appereth in ye rolle of her accounte
iiij li. viij. d.

On the 22nd July, the 31st year of King Henry VI. (1452), regulations to the following effect were " avised and ordeined " for the fraternity of our Lady by the advice of Richard Aley, Alderman and Master of Corpus Christi, and the wardens of the same, with the xvi chosen of the fraternity of our Lady.

That no person being brother of the fraternity that happeneth to fall to poverty shall be received into the alms of the fraternity without the counsel of the like authorities for the time being.

That the priests of the fraternity shall have the livery that the wardens shall ordain for a gown cloth, paying only 4d. a-year to the wardens.

That the four wardens of the brotherhood of our Lady shall yearly give up their accounts on the 12th July before the master and wardens and fellowship of the said craft under pain of £10 to the increase of the box of the brotherhood.

The four wardens shall not present or take in any brother or sister " by way of pardon, but if it be þe wifs of þe seid wardeins p^t for þe tyme shul be, oonly."

That if any bequest or other gift be given to the worship of our Lady and helping of the brotherhood, the wardens shall bring them in, whole, beside their account of receipts and payments.

At the end of the succeeding year follows this entry, showing that the rule took effect :—

These beñ the hole bequests in þe said wardens time to þe vse of þe said brethered.

Alsoñ Pangbourne late oon of þe Almes women of þe said brethered hath goven in worship of our lady & augmentyng of þe said ffrat'nite in mony xxs.

Item, j dussen Sponys of Silver weyng xiij unc' & j qrt' of troy weight.

Item, j bordcloth of diap' conteynyng vj yerdis.

Item, j towell of diap' cont' x yerdis & iij qrt'.

Item, halfe a dussein of countrefete vessell.

Item, j basoñ & an ewer of laton.

The extensive lists of names of members of the fraternity snow that it was by no means confined to Londoners, nor to persons in the trade of Skinners; thus, for example, in 1445, we find several resident at Reigate, and others at St. Alban's, Wednesbury, Bristowe, Haselingfield, Charlwood, Salisbury, Aldenham, and Godstone; and among the descriptions are doctor, gentleman, butcher, dyer, joiner, grocer, and silkwife.

Opposite to the list dated the 11th Edward IV. (1471) is noted the enrolment of the queen, thus—

Our moost goode and graciouse Quene Elisabeth, Soster vnto this oure ffraternite, Of oure blissed lady, And moder of mercy, sanct mary virgyn the moder of God.

And in 1475 are the following:—

The Qween Margarete sūtyme wyff and spowse to kyng Harry the sexthe.
My lady Vawys, dam kat'ine.
Maistresse Elyanore Hawte with the Qween.
Maistyr John Holcot.
Alys Holcot his wyff w^t þ^e queē.
Sir Jamys Walkere p'st of seÿt Johñs in walbroke.

and several described as gentleman, draper, flecher, tailor, and brewer, besides skinners.

These examples will suffice to show the reputation of the fraternity to be such that the highest persons in the realm were enrolled in the list of members.

The entries are continued year by year with the greatest regularity, enlivened with illuminated capitals, and occasionally with a large miniature of some member of very special distinction.

The last record of the enrolment of new sisters occurs in the year 1542, when five were elected.

On the 20th July in the third year of King Edward VI (1549) the names are entered as the brethren of our Lady's Assumption in the time of certain wardens of the fraternity, but in the fifth year they are called "the bretheren of the yeomanry of the Skinners."

In 1561 occurs the following entry:—

Be it remembered that Mr. Thomas Persie (late master 1553), hathe of his lyberalite geven unto the use of the Copany of Skinners of London a tabellw^t a fframe at ye upp, onde of the hall and a fayre carpet to ye same w^t his armes, also a tabell cloth an towell of damaske worke to the same.

Two of the pages or skins of this volume, which are in size about

The Qween Margarete sittÿ
me wyff and Spolble to kÿng
Harry the sethe.

Illumination from the Books of the Skinners Company A.D. 1422.

sixteen inches by eleven, contain drawings of a more elaborate character. In one we have the assumption of the Virgin, who appears in an attitude of adoration, with hands folded in prayer, looking as it were to heaven, while the three Persons of the blessed Trinity are about to place a crown upon her head. On either side are angels with expanded wings, one on the right hand holds an ermine cap or crown, and the other the monogram IMR.; the Virgin is encompassed with a nimbus as well as the Trinity. She is robed in a purple mantle, powdered with stars and lined with ermine, and wears underneath a pink dress, deeply flounced with the same material. Below a figure is represented as kneeling, and a label issuing from her mouth is inscribed with the words " Soi dei genitas ou," and the following laudatory dedication :

Ascendit Xp'us sup' celos et preparauit sue castissime matri immortalitatis locum et hoc est illa preclara festiuitas omn' sanctor' festiuitatib' incomparabilis in qua gloriosa et felix intrantib' celestis curie ordinib' ad etherum peruenit thalamum quo pia sui memorum immemor nequaquam existat. T' Exaltata es sancta dei genetrix super coros angelorum ad celestia regna.

Deus qui birginalem aulam in qua habitares eligere dignatus es da quesumus ut sua nos defensione munitos ibruudos faciat sue interesse festibitati qui nunc et regna cum deo patre in unitate spiritus sancti deus p' omnia secula seculo'. Amen.

The Guild roll on the opposite page shows it to have been executed in the sixth year of Henry VII. A.D. 1491.

On the other, Lady Elizabeth Grey, the wife of Edward IV. is represented standing in a commanding attitude, with the ball and sceptre in her hands, and a regal crown upon her head; the expression is sweet and placid, and her hair, which is of a light flaxen colour, falls gracefully over her shoulders; she is robed in purple with a golden border; the robe is lined with ermine, as well as the bodice and skirt, which are of a crimson colour. The background is tastefully filled with roses and pinks, gracefully wreathed together, and the whole encompassed with an illuminated border, with the dedication already referred to:

Oure moost goode and graciouse Quene Elisabeth, Soster buto this oure fraternite. Of oure blissed lady and modr of mercy Sanct Mary birgyn the modr of God.

The date given on the opposite page is that of the 11th of Edward IV. A.D. 1471.

The extracts and notes above given are those of the most interest and importance, and serve to illustrate the value and curious contents of the early records belonging to the Company, which would well merit a far more extended notice.

SKINNERS' HALL.

Herbert, quoting from Stowe,[1] says there is an old record that the original hall of the Company "consisted of iiij small tenements in the parish of St. John's upon Walbrocke, and ij tenements in St. Martyn's Orgar, and that they had licence of King Henry III. for the same;" the rent per annum is mentioned as xii. vi. viii.; this was afterwards alienated, although by what means is uncertain, and in the 19th of Edward II. was the property of Ralph de Cobham, who, having made Edward the Third his heir, put it in that monarch's power to restore to the Company their ancient hall, at the same time that he granted them a charter, and allowed his illustrious name to be added to the guild. (1327).

Of the original building known as Copped Hall nothing now remains save some of the old walls, which were sufficiently substantial to resist the Fire in 1666. I have not been able to find a plan of the first building, but the four small buildings were no doubt facing Dowgate Hill. The frontage to the street is 50 feet. There was a court or quadrangle somewhat similar to the present, and the entrance direct into the hall. The present building appears to have been erected as soon as the funds of the Company enabled them to rebuild after the Fire.

At this time the Company held their courts at other places, as we find the Salters kindly lending their hall. Courts also appear to have been held at the Bull Inn in Bishopsgate, and also in the church of St. Helen's.

Soon after the fire the rubbish and old lead were sold, and a Committee appointed (Oct. 15, 1668) for the purpose of carrying out the rebuilding of the Hall. Sir George Waterman, knt., Master, with Sir Thomas Pilkington and others, were on the Committee. In Nov. 1668, it was ordered that the front houses at Skinners' Hall should be rebuilt, "with what speed they conveniently may, and the Warden

[1] Stowe, i. 201.

Gibbs, Mr. Rodgers, Mr. Smith, and others be a Committee to find and bye what timber, deals, lyme, ironwork, at the best and fittest season, and in what quantities, they shall think fit."

In February the Renter was empowered to make the gateway of stone or timber as he thought fit, the quadrangle to be 40 ft. square. Shortly afterwards we find the Renter reports a want of money; to meet this difficulty the Master and Wardens advanced 1000*l.* at 6 per cent., and every member was pledged to use his influence to raise a like sum for the use of the Company. Other means were also resorted to for raising funds, viz., by summoning 20 or more yeomen and bachelors to take upon them the livery or clothing of the Company, the fee of which was 15*l.*, and in case of refusal fining the unfortunate member 20*l.*

We next hear of the Hall being plastered. At a Court held June 28th, 1670, a screen is ordered for the hall, and the windows of the Court-room to be wainscoted with what speed they may be. On Oct. 6, 1671, Renter Gibbs and others were ordered to view the Hall to see if it may be fitted up by Lord Mayor's day.[1] It must have been completed in 1672, as it was let to Sir George Waterman during his year of office as mayor from the 1st of November 1672 to the 1st of November 1673, at a rental of 160*l.* per annum. The description of the procession[2] starting from the Hall at 7 o'clock in the morning is to be found in Herbert's History of the Twelve Companies.[3]

In 1678 the Court ordered a parlour to be erected with a room over it behind the Hall and an attic. Two of these now form Committee Rooms. The carving over the chimney-piece in the Court and Cedar Withdrawing Room is carefully executed in the best style of Grinling Gibbons. In 1691 the New East India Company held the first meetings here. Macaulay in his Hist. of England[4] speaks of it:

The Skinners built their stately Hall, and the meetings were held in a parlour, renowned for the fragrance which exhaled from a magnificent wainscot of cedar. * * * * * * *

During the summer of 1691 the controversy which raged between the Leaden-

---

[1] In this year the Court authorised the Wardens' disposal of certain surplus land in the rear of the Hall at 3*d.* per foot, which we find was afterwards sold to Mr. Fairbrother.

[2] Towards which the Company subscribed £200.

[3] P. 321.

[4] Macaulay, vol. iv. cap. xviii. p. 144, &c.

hall Street Company and the Dowgate Company kept the City in constant agitation, and the Parliament no sooner met than both parties presented petitions to the House of Commons. * * * * *

The tracts which the rival bodies put forth were innumerable if the drama of that age is to be trusted. The feud between the India House and Skinners' Hall was for some time as serious an impediment to the course of true love in London as the feud between the Capulets and Montagues had been at Verona.

The play which Macaulay alludes to is given in a note:

Hast thou been bred up like a virtuous and sober maiden, and wouldest thou take the part of a profane wretch who sold his stock out of the Old East India Company?

It was in consequence of these meetings that the New Company on its amalgamation with the Old presented the Skinners' Company with a carved mahogany court table and silver candlesticks.

Two small statuettes in the drawing-room are worthy of attention, being representations of Edward III.[1] and Sir Andrew Judd.

On the staircase is a full-length portrait of Sir Thomas Pilkington.

In the court-room is a portrait of Sir Joseph Causton, knight, and one of T. G. Kensit, Esq. (the present worthy clerk) by Richmond, R.A., and a small portrait which is said to be that of Sir Andrew Judd. Also a view of Tonbridge School, painted by T. S. Wells, Esq., Master, 1836.

The façade of the Hall next the street is somewhat like that of old Covent Garden Theatre in the time of Garrick. It was erected under the superintendence of the Company's surveyor, Douswell, A.D. 1777. Some alterations to the Hall were made by Mr. Jupp, afterwards surveyor to the Company, but the present roof was from a design of Mr. George Moore, architect, and has been recently redecorated under the superintendence of the Company's present surveyor, Mr. Edward Henry Burnell.

In concluding my remarks on the Company's Hall I would fain adopt the words of Stowe, who, after describing the history of the Company, adds, "Thus much to stop the tongue of unthankful men, such as used to ask, Why have ye not noted this, or that? and give

[1] There is a striking resemblance between this statuette and an engraving in the *Hist. of British Costumes* published by Knight, which is taken from an initial letter in the Grant of the Duchy of Acquitaine.—*Library of Entertaining Knowledge* by Knight, p. 137.

no thanks for what is done; but I feel my inadequacy to the task I have undertaken and crave your indulgence for my omissions."

The arms which had been previously used were confirmed, and the "crest and bestes" (*i.e.* supporters) of the Company, granted by Thomas Hawley, Clarencieux King-of-Arms, on the 1st October, 4 Edward VI. entered and approved at the Visitation in 1634, John Benet, Master. The shield is—Ermine, on a chief gules three ducal coronets or, capped of the field and tasselled gold. The crest is a lizard[1] statant ppr. gorged with a wreath, leaved vert, purfflied or. The supporters are—Dexter, a lizard ppr. sinister, a martin sable, each gorged with a wreath, leaved vert. In the old court-books the motto is, "In Christo Fratres," and it is not until the year 1687 that we find the present motto of the Company adopted, viz.

"To God only be all Glory."

THE BARGE.[2]

[NOTE.—All extracts from Stowe are from Strype's edition, printed 1720.]

The Skinners, in common with others of the City Guilds, had their state barge in which they were wont to take part in City pageants, accompanying my Lord Mayor on the occasion of his proceeding by water to Westminster on the festival of St. Simon and St. Jude (old style), when he took the customary oaths in the Court of Exchequer, before the Lord Chancellor. They likewise escorted him back to Guildhall with banners, streamers, trumpets, kettledrums, and haut-boys.

Although the custom of the Lord Mayor's taking the oath of allegiance at Westminster dates back as early as the year 1250, it appears that up to the year 1453 the procession was on horseback.[3] In the year last mentioned[4] Sir John Norman was elected Mayor, and he caused a barge to be built at his own costs and charges in which he proceeded in state to Westminster, and the Companies had several barges well decked and manned to pass along with him. This made the Lord Mayor very popular, especially so with the

---

[1] I am reminded by G. E. Cokayne, Esq. *Lancaster Herald*, that the lizard is almost the same as the leopard, and is generally so depicted, but that it is brown and with a short tail. Edmonson says it is "a short-tailed cat of Norway," and this is what it probably is. In some documents the word is "lazarde."

[2] Stowe, vol. i. p. 169. [3] Knight's *London*, p. 7.

[4] Fairholt, *City Pageants*, tells us that a barge was hired fifteen years previously. A.D. 1435.

watermen, and they celebrated the event in a song, which was composed and sung to a lively air, commencing with these words:

Row thy boat Norman, row to thy leman.

In 1482 the convenience of this arrangement was further improved by Sir John Shaw, or Shaa, who proceeded to and from Westminster by water.

On royal and state occasions also the City Companies attended the Lord Mayor. When Henry VII. willed the coronation of his Queen Elizabeth she was brought from Greenwich by barges all freshly furnished with banners and silk streamers.

When Henry VIII. avowed his marriage with Anne Boleyn she was brought by all the craft of London from Greenwich to the Tower, trumpets, shawms, and other instruments all the way making play and great melody ; also when Queen Henrietta arrived in London June 16th, 1625, the King and Queen in the royal barge, with many other barges of honour, and thousands of boats, passed through London Bridge. Again, in 1662, to quote the words of Evelyn : [1]

I was spectator of the most magnificent triumph that ever floated on the Thames, considering the innumerable boats and vessels, dress'd and adorn'd with all imaginable pomp, but above all the thrones, arches, pageants, and other stately representations, stately barges of the Lord Mayor and Companies, with various inventions, musiq, and peales of ordnance, both from ye vessells and ye shore, going to meet and conduct the new queene from Hampton Court to Whitehall, at her first time of coming to towne. In my opinion, it far exceeded all ye Venetian Bucentoras, &c., on the occasion when they go to espouse the Adriatic. His Matie and the Queene came in an antique shaped vessell, covered with a stall or canopy of cloth of gold, made in form of a cupola, supported with high Corinthian pillars, wreathed with flowers, festoons, and garlands ; I was in our new built vessell sailing amongst them.

A picture representing the pageant is now in Her Majesty's collection.

In June 1728 the Company's barge was reported out of repair, and a committee was appointed to obtain tenders for the construction of a new barge, or if possible the repair of the old one. At this time the Company for economical reasons ordered the repairs to the extent of 25*l*. Mr. Richard Bernard, the builder, undertaking to keep her afloat for ten years more. The specification of Bernard appears to have been entered in extenso in the Court Books. As it affords some curious information concerning the construction and cost of a barge at that time, I venture to insert it.[2]

---

[1] Memoirs, vol. i. p. 352. See also Aqua Triumphalis, engraved by John Tatham, folio, 1662. [2] Court Books, August 14th, 1728.

THE COMPANY OF SKINNERS.

Mr. Richard Bernard's Estimate for building a new Barge.

For building a new barge, the length to be 73 ffoot and three inches.
The width of the fordpart of the house is 10 foot 10 wide.
The depth of the fordpart of the house is three foot.
The length of the house from bulkhead to bulkhead, thirty and four foot, and four inches or thereabouts.
The width of the barge in the middle of the house is eleven feet and 6 inches.
The width of the barge in the after bulkhead is 10 ft. 5 inches.
The depth at the after part of the house is four feet six inches.

The hull of the aforesaid barge to be built with inch board and three-quarter inch board, and the timbers to be three inches in thickness, to be cut out of English oak. The said hull of the barge comes to £100.

The house to be thirty-four feet in length with lockers, and seats and wainscotting, with hinges and locks.

Thirty-six looking glass plates to be diamond cut for the sashes.

The fore bulkhead, ten foot and a half and six foot four inches high, or thereabouts, with fflouted piloustcd pilasters with carved captols.

The bulkhead shall be eleven foot wide and five foot ten inches high; four carved elbows for the seats in the State Rooms.

Two fflouted columns to support the beam, four carved brackets at the corners of the house, pail boards to be carved.

The shield to be nine inches thick with the Company's coat of arms to taffrail of the said barge.

The ceiling of the barge to be good seasoned yellow deals.

The rails of the house four inches broad and one inch ¼ thick.

Six handsome wainsscotte fformes.

A plank with iron work sufficient for the sashes, to be silk, blew or red.

The said work comes to £110.

To guild the carved quarter, pairds, large shield in the starn, the carved bracketts in the ffront, and back part of the house, the pillasters, between the sashes, the flouted pillasters with their capitols and bases, the King's arms in the Master's seat, and other figures as is proper, and the inside of the house varnished with white spirit varnish, and all other ornaments painted and guilded at £36 15 0

For eighteen new ashen oars for the barge . . .	9	0	0
For a hitcher, staff, and hook	0	2	0
For one hundred yards of vittory for the covering of the barge, at 12*d.* per yard, complatly sowed together after the best manner	5	0	0
	50	17	0
The hull of the said barge	100	0	0
The building of the house complcatly finished	110	0	0
	£260	17	0

c 2

Ten years having passed since the last-mentioned repairs, the Court decided upon building a new barge, and, having heard that Mr. Hall had recently constructed barges for other of the City Companies, they appointed a time to meet Mr. Hall and view the Fishmongers' barge. The result was that they contracted with Mr. Hall to build them one of the same dimensions, but with certain alterations as to the gilded images, for the sum of 439*l*.; and Mr. Thomas Nash, then Master, was desired to provide glass and other furniture similar to the Fishmongers'. On the following May, 1739, the barge was prepared for the reception of the Members of the Court and their ladies.

On the election of Sir George Mertins as Mayor in 1724, eight poor men with quarter-staffs were ordered to attend the procession; twenty rich bachelors to walk before the Company in velvet coats, gold chains, and white staffs; the Company to provide gloves, and 2s. 6d. to be allowed for their dinner.

When Sir Charles Asgill was elected Lord Mayor in 1757,[1] a Master of Defence with eight men were substituted for the eight men with quarter-staffs, and fifty with javelins, a gentleman usher, thirty pensioners with gold chains; thirty whifflers with a star had 3s. each and 1s. for dinner, and eight sweepers with brooms had the same.

Again, on the election of Sir R. Kite, Skinner, to the office of Mayor in 1776,[1] the Company's barge was ordered out, repainted and gilded, the Company mustering in force. A new silk gown was ordered for the barge-master, new scarf for his mate, jackets and caps for the men, fifty-eight gowns and caps for pensioners, thirty gold chains for the gentlemen, cockades and ribbons without stint, and none of the livery were admitted without a gown. The most singular entry is for John Wade, master of defence, who was to provide eight men with eight bells, with scarves and cockades, to form part of the procession.

The barge was used by the sheriff in 1775, and appears to have met with some damage at a regatta in 1776;[2] it was repaired at an expense of £21 16s. 0d. in 1777.

In 1783 the Lord Mayor was informed that the Company's barge was again out of repair, and they desired to be excused from taking part in the procession to Westminster. It was afterwards repaired by Searle, in 1785; and with few exceptions the Skinners continued to

[1] Court Books.
[2] For a silver cup of 20 guineas, given by the Duke of Cumberland. Ann. Register.

accompany the Lord Mayor on his way to and from Westminster, until it was finally disused. In the year 1786 there is an entry to the effect that no French wines or hock be drank on board the barge. In 1827 it was put into thorough repair by Messrs. Rawlinson and Lyon, at a cost of £665.

On the occasion of the opening of New London Bridge by His Majesty King William IV. and Queen Adelaide, August 1st, 1831, Sir John Key, Bart., Mayor, and the whole of the Corporation and City Companies were present in their gorgeous state barges, while craft of all descriptions gaily dressed with flags covered the river. A channel was kept open for the royal procession, by means of vessels and barges moored alongside, extending in two lines from Somerset House to London Bridge, the arrangement of which had been confided to Admiral Sir Byam Martin.

On the occasion of Her Majesty honouring the City with her presence, at the opening of the New Coal Exchange, October 23, 1849, the Skinners and other Companies in their barges attended Her Majesty in her progress to the Custom House, and also again accompanied her back to Whitehall.

The barge was repaired again in 1855 by Mr. Cristal, when the Company spent £257 14s. upon it.

In consequence of the Lord Mayor and other Companies putting down their barges, the Company unwillingly gave up theirs. It was sold in 1858 to Mr. Searle for £75, and the old hull may still be seen floating on the river at the side of the Christ Church meadows at Oxford.

The Company usually set apart one day in the year for an excursion to Richmond, when every member of the Court had the privilege of taking with him on the barge two ladies, or one lady and one gentleman. The start was from Dyers' Hall Wharf, and in later times from Waterloo Bridge, where the Company embarked about 11 A.M., and with eighteen rowers proceeded with the tide as far as Putney; here the barge stopped at Mr. Michael Turner's, and other members of the Company joined them; afterwards re-embarking, a light luncheon of fruit and ices was served, and the band enlivened the rest of the voyage with a choice selection of instrumental music. Arriving at Richmond they proceeded to the Star and Garter Hotel, where an elegant entertainment was provided. At 8 P.M. or soon after, those who preferred it returned by water, and pleasant was it for the visitors and younger members of the Company to dance on the deck by moonlight, while the barge glided gently on, and the sound of the band was wafted over the still waters of the Thames, or sitting with their seniors in the saloon to hear glees and madrigals. As the barge grounded at Putney the rippling tide beat on her clincher-built sides, and flowing onwards swept away with the commingled cadence of the well-known glee—

> "Sleep, gentle lady, the flowers are closing,
> The very winds and waves reposing;
> Sleep while we sing good night,
> Good night! good night!
> Good night!"

One other custom deserves notice. When the Lord Mayor had landed at Westminster, the barges of the Skinners and Merchant Taylors were brought alongside each other, when ample store of cakes and wine were produced. The wine was drunk from wooden bowls, and the Master and Wardens of the Skinners drank to the health of the Master and Wardens of the Merchant Taylors, root and branch, and might they continue for ever. This loving toast was responded to by the Merchant Taylors in good fellowship and in remembrance of the decree of Sir Richard Billesden as before-mentioned.

One of the best drawings of a City barge (the Stationers) is given in *Shipping and Craft*, published A.D. 1829, by E. W. Cook, Esq., R.A. The men's caps were of red velvet, trimmed round the head with ermine, and expanding to a square at the top in a somewhat similar manner to the University form; in front of each was a silver leopard, the crest of the Company; they had also blue striped cotton shirts and trowsers; the barge-master's coat was scarlet, of true waterman's cut, with ample pleated skirt, ermine collar and cuffs, and the shield of the Company, in silver blazoned, on the left arm. Red smalls and stockings. Eighteen men were employed as rowers; one at the bow seated on a leopard had a boat-hook, and two at the helm, completed the crew.

The Skinners' and Goldsmiths' Companies conjointly rented a barge-house at Chelsea of the Archbishop of Canterbury, afterwards of the Apothecaries' Company.

CITY PAGEANTS.

Stowe mentions the names of twenty-one lord mayors as being members of the Company. The earliest is Sir Thomas Leggy, 1348, 1355. The last Sir Richard Chiverton, 1658: besides these I have traced numerous others who will be referred to hereafter in a list of such members of our Company as have filled this important office.[1]

Of the city pageants six are mentioned by Herbert as described and printed.

The First, that of Sir Wolstan Dixie, is to be found in Stowe, acted Oct. 29, 1585; a copy in black letter, 4to. imprinted by Joseph Alde, by George Peele, M.A., Oxon., is in the Bodleian Library.

The Second is the Triumph of Love and Antiquity, by Thomas Middleton, imprinted by Nicholas Oatres, 1619; it was acted before Sir William Cokayne, Oct. 29, 1619, wherein he is thus addressed by Orpheus—

> Behold yon bird of state, the vigilant cock,
> The morning herald and the plowman's clock,
> At whoes shrill crow the very lion trembles;
> The hardest prey of all that here assembles;
> How fitly do's it match your name and power,
> First by that name; now is this glorious hour.
> At your first voyce, to shake the bold'st offence
> And sturdiest sin, that 'ere had residence
> In sane man, yet with an equal eie
> Watching grave justice, with fair clemency,
> It being the property he chiefly shows,
> To give wing warning still before he crows;
> To crow before he strikes, with his clapt wing;
> To stir himself up first, which needful thing
> Is every man's first duty by his crow:
> A gentle call, or warning, which should show
> From every Magistrate, ere he extend
> The stroke of justice, he should apprehend;
> If that prevail not, then the spur—the *Sword*.

The Third.—London's Triumph, by J. B., 4to.; no copy either in the British Museum or City Library. The pageant took place when Sir Robert Titchborne was Mayor 1656.

The Fourth.—Londinum Triumphans, by J. Tathan, a well-known dramatist, celebrated 29th Oct. 1657, in honour of the truly deserving

---

[1] Three of these served the office of Lord Mayor twice, and one, viz. Pilkington, three times.

Richard Chiverton, Lord Mayor of London, done at the cost and charges of the Worshipful Company of Skinners. A copy was sold at Mr. West's sale, but present possessor is unknown. There is no copy either in the British Museum or Guildhall Library.

The Fifth.—London's Resurrection to Joy and Triumph expressed in sundry shows, shapes, scenes, speeches, and songs, in parts celebrious to the much merited magistrate Sir George Waterman, knt. Lord Mayor of the City of London, at the peculiar and proper expense of the Worshipful Company of Skinners. Written by Thomas Jordan, London: printed for Henry Brown at the Gun, in St. Paul's Churchyard, 1671. Extracts are given by Herbert and Strype:[1] a copy is in the Guildhall Library. The following extract may not prove uninteresting.

The Skinners met at the Hall at seven o'clock and formed in procession. The address to Sir George Waterman commences thus:

> In the first Age, when Innocence began
> To spread her splendour on the Soul of Man,
> Union filled all the universe with free
> Felicious and seraphic Harmony;
> All parts of the Creation did consent,
> And the world was one well-tuned Instrument;
> Dog, Bear, Wolf, Lamb, together did agree,
> Nature itself knew no antipathy;
> But, when the peace was broke by Man's Transgression,
> Revenge with rage and envy took possession;
> Discord rioted, and in conclusion
> Old Amnesty was turned into confusion.

The Sixth.—London's Great Triumph, restored and performed on Tuesday the 29th, 1689, for the entertainment of the Right Honourable Sir Thomas Pilkington, knt. Lord Mayor of the City of London; containing a description of the several pageants and speeches, together with a song for the entertainment of their Majesties, who with their Royal Highnesses the Prince and Princess of Denmark, the whole Court, and both Houses of Parliament, honoured his Lordship this year with their presence. All set forth at the proper costs and charges of the Right Worshipful Company of Skinners by Matthew Tautman.

Londinum Urbs Sinclita Regum. London, printed for Langley Curtis at Sir Edmundsbury Godfrey's head, near Fleet Street Bridge, 1689.

[1] Vol. ii. 325.

THE COMPANY OF SKINNERS. 41

The Seventh, not mentioned by Strype in his edition of Stow or Herbert in his *History of the Twelve Great Companies*, is as follows:—

Sir Anthony Bateman, Master of the Skinners' Company, and Lord Mayor of the city of London 1665.

A pageant was enacted called "London's Triumph," at the cost and charges of the Worshipful Company of Skinners.

The procession started from Skinners' Hall at 8 o'clock A.M.

First. Master and Wardens in their gowns faced with foyne.

Secondly. The Livery in gowns faced with budge.

Thirdly. Forty foyne Bachelors in gowns and satin hoods.

Fourthly. Fifty Bachelors in gowns and satin hoods.

Fifthly. Fifty budge Bachelors in gowns and satin hoods.

Sixthly. Other gentlemen carrying banners and colours of the Company ; 11 of them in plush.

Seventhly. Sergeant Trumpeter and 35 Trumpeters; 16 of His Majesty's Servants, and 4 of the Duke of Albemarle's.

The Drum-Major and 4 more of His Majesty's Drums.

7 other Drums.

A Fife.

2 more Fifes.

All except His Majesty's Sergeants habited in buff-colored doublets, black hose, and scarfs about their waists.

2 City Marshalls.

The Foot Marshall.

70 Pensioners in red gowns, red sleeves, and red caps, each with a javelin in one hand and a target in the other, whereon is painted the coat of arms of their benefactors.

All with the Company's colors in their hats.

The pageant is made in the manner of a wood or wilderness, being 14 feet long and 8 feet broad. The front thereof is arched over with a wild arbour, whereon sits a figure representing Faunus. His head is clothed with wool intermixed with ermine, the upper part of his body habited like a forester in green, and his nether part like a woodman in russet ; in one hand he holds a javelin, and in the other a bugle-horn; his attendants are three satyrs, playing on rude instruments. Upon 4 pedestals sit 4 girls, nymphs of the forest called Dryads, and habited accordingly. On the stage are placed several boys habited as bears, monkeys, and several other beasts relating to the Company's trades. Upon the approach of the Mayor the faun thus addresses him :—

> Ere scarce the force of government was known,
> Or superstitious ceremony shown;
> Ere Rome received from Romulus her law,
> Which did the Sabines to subjection draw,
> Or that the gods into request became,
> And altars on her Holy Mount did flame,
> I led the way to those mysterious rites,
> By the pale tapers of instructive lights;

> For Nature (then), as Heathen reason lent,
> To worship what we call Omnipotent,
> Where now the one, as oft strives to deface,
> With oaths and blasphemy the seat of Grace,
> Worser than Heathen slaves, past sense of shame,
> From Christian into Atheist change their name;
> We were devout in what we did not know;
> They know, and yet they will not devotion show;
> In woods and groves at first we sacrificed,
> And then we temples to erect devised;
> As we grew up in knowledge, we the more
> Our unknown God did honor and adore;
> These sort of men your temples do despise,
> And to the beasts do only sacrifice;
> That such who thus your government displease
> Deserve the name of satyrs more than these.
> Licentious liberty, obdurate hearts,
> And men from virtue more than beast departs;
> For they forsake not their's, and, as we do,
> Order our beasts, let them be ordered too.
> Wild beasts are tamed by reason, and wild men may
> Be brought in time to be as tame as they;
> "Tis wisdom in the magistrate that must
> Crumble all such prejudices into dust.
> Let such as in your Church no service love
> Confined be in a forest, wood, or grove;
> Let them be company for beasts, not men,
> Till they return unto the truth again;
> By this their punishment you will appear
> Unto the world more virtuous than severe."

As he proceeded other speeches were addressed to him—

1. By Albion;
2. By a Turk;
3. By Minerva;
4. By a Turk again at Guildhall;

which ended, his Lordship entered his house, all depart in order (as the conveniency of night will admit), and the several persons appointed to attend the service of the day take especial care to lodge the silk hoods and triumphs in some secure place, until they can remove them to Skinners' Hall; in regard they are of some weight, for the burden of the day (adds the historian) was great upon the undertakers.—Printed by Roger le Strange, 1663.[1]

---

[1] It is worthy of remark that Monk, Duke of Albemarle, was entertained by the Skinners when he supported the claims of Charles II., on which occasion the royal arms were replaced, first in the Company's Hall, and afterwards in the City, where they had been banished during the time of the Commonwealth.

MEMBERS OF THE COMPANY WHO ALSO SERVED THE OFFICE OF MAYOR IN THE CITY OF LONDON.

The following list, containing a few brief notices of the historical incidents relating to some of the ancient worthies of the Company who have served the office of Lord Mayor of the City of London, may not be uninteresting.

I am indebted for the blazon of the coats of arms to John de Havilland, Esq. F.S.A. York Herald.

THOMAS LEGGE, or LEGGY, Mayor A.D. 1347, 1355, M.P. 20 Edward III.

Arms: Vert, a buck's head or, on a chief argent three crosses flory azure.[1]

He bequeathed 100*l.* for cleaning fosses, on condition that masses were offered for his soul in the Chapel of St. Mary, Guildhall.[2] He also gave 300*l.* to Edw. III. to assist in the expedition against France during his Mayoralty. He married Elizabeth, daughter of Thomas Beauchamp, Earl of Warwick. Their son John Legg was a farmer of the public revenue, and serjeant-at-arms to King Richard II. He took part in the insurrection of Wat Tyler, and was beheaded, together with Simon Sudbury, Archbishop of Canterbury, Robert Hales, Prior of the Hospital of St. John of Jerusalem, and others, on Tower Hill, on the 14th June, 1381. His father, the mayor, who, Stowe says, was the sufferer on this occasion, had however been dead many years before.[3] Their immediate ancestors are said to have descended from a patrician family in the city of Bavonna, in Italy, who settled in England about the time of King Henry II.

---

[1] In Harl. MSS. 1049 and 1349 the arms are Azure, a buck's head cabossed or, on a chief argent three crosses moline of the first (thus in Harl. MSS. 1049, fo. 39). Heylyn's Help, 1773, gives the same blazon. Harl. MSS. 1349, fol. 6b, blazons the coat in the same way, except that the field is stated to be vert.

[2] Sargeant's *Lord Mayors of London*, MS. Guildhall.

Corporation Records. Letter Books, G. fol. 163; H. fols. 21 and 133.

ADAM OF BURY, temp. Edw. III., twice Mayor, 1364, 1373.

Arms: Quarterly, ermine and azure, in second and third quarters an eagle or falcon rising or.[1]

Letter extant in City Records from Johanna announcing the birth of a son, Edward Prince of Gascoyne and of Wales, 1365.

He was buried in old St. Paul's, and made a provision in his will, A.D. 1373, that out of his estate three chaplains should say mass in a certain chapel, at that time new built, near the north door, behind the cross, for the health of his soul and all faithful souls deceased; this property was assigned by his executors to the Dean and Chapter of St. Paul's.

Sir HENRY BARTON, Knt., Lord Mayor of London A.D. 1417, 1429, temp. Henry V. and VI.

Arms: Erm. on a saltire sable an annulet or, voided of the field.

To Sir Henry Barton, Citizen and Skinner, the City of London is indebted for having first introduced a system of lighting. He ordained that lanthorns should be hung out in the City between Hallowmas E'en and Candlemas; besides these every constable in London had his cresset or lanthorn; the charge for which was in lights ij s. iiij d.; each cresset had two men, one to bear or hold it, and another to carry a bag with lights to serve it. There were about 2,000 men so employed; every one beside his wages had his breakfast and was furnished with a straw hat, on which a number was conspicuously displayed; 500 cressets were furnished by the City companies, and the remaining 200 by the Chamber of London.[2]

By his will [3] the testator gave to William Newenham, master of the guild or fraternity of the precious body of our Lord Jesus Christ, and to John Beale and others, wardens of the said fraternity, and to the brethren and sisters of the same guild or fraternity, and to the men of the said mystery, and to Mr. Wm. Kirkeby, rector of the church of St. John upon Walbrook, London, and to their suc-

[1] See Harl. MSS. 1049 and 1349.
[2] Stowe, ii. 256.
[3] Herbert.

cessors, master, wardens, rector, and their successors for ever, all his tenement, with the mansions, houses, shops, cellars, and their appurtenances, in Watling Street, in the parish of Aldermarie Chirche, of London; all his tenement, with the appurtenances, in the parish of Allhallows in Bread Street, London, on the north part of the street called Watling Street, to grant and let to poor and needy persons who heretofore held houses and maintained families, and had by divine visitation and adverse fortune come to extreme want, receiving nothing from them for the habitations aforesaid."

Also, he gave and devised to the master, wardens, brethren, and sisters aforesaid, and to the rectors of the said church and their successors, all the tenement with appurtenances, and the great garden with the repairs to the said tenement, situate and being over against the hospital of the Blessed Mary without Bishopsgate, in the suburbs of London, to hold the same to them and their successors for ever, upon condition of their completing all his ordinances above-mentioned; and if they should make default then he gave the same to the mayor and chamberlain and their successors as aforesaid.

He is said to have been "buried in the charnell house by Pauls, on the north side of the churchyard, now pulled downe and dwelling houses erected in the place thereof."[1]

Sir WILLIAM GREGORY, son of Roger Gregory of Mildenhall, Suffolk, Mayor A.D. 1451, temp. Henry VI. He was buried in the church of St. Ann by Aldersgate.

Arms: Per pale arg. and az. two lions ramp. endorsed counterchanged.

Sir THOMAS OLDGRAVE, or OULEGREVE, son of William Oldgrave of Knottysford, in Cheshire, Mayor 1467, temp. Edward IV.; taken prisoner by the Earl of Warwick and brought to London.

Arms: Az. a fess engr. erm. between three owls or.

During his mayoralty Dame Margaret, sister unto the King, rode through the city on

[1] Harl. MSS. 1349, fo. 12.

her way to the sea-side to pass into Flanders, there to be married to Charles Duke of Burgundy. After whose departure "Sir Thos. Cooke, late Mair (A.D 1462), which before was peached of treason by a servant of Lord Wenlock's called Hawkins, at the request of the said Lady Margaret upon suretie suffered to go at large, was arrested and sent unto the Tower, and his goods seized by the Lord Rivers, then Treasurer of England; and his wife put out of the house, and committed to the charge of the Mair, in whose place she lay for a season.

"Sir Thos. was brought into Guildhall and there arreined of the said treason, and after that committed to the Countoure in Bread Street, and from thence to the King's Bench in Southwarke. In which time and season he lost much good, for both his places in the countrie and also in London were under ye guiding of the said Lord Rivers' servants, and of Sir John Fog, the under-treasurer; the which spoyled and distroyed much things; and over that much of his jeweles and plate, with greate substance of ye merchandise, as cloth of silk and clothes of arras, were discovered by such persons as he had betaken ye said goods to kepe, and came to the treasurer's hands, which to the said Sir Thomas was a great enemy, and finally, after many persecutions and losses, was compelled as for fine to pay unto the King 8,000*l.*; and after he had thus agreed, and was at large, for the King's interest, he was then in new trouble against the Queene, which demanded as her right for every 1,000*l.* paid unto the King by way of fine 100 markes, to which he was fain to agree, besides many good gifts that he gave to his council." [1]

Sir WILLIAM MARTIN, son of Walter Martin of Hertford, Mayor 1492, temp. Henry VII.

Arms: Or, two bars gules, in the dexter chief an escutcheon erm.[2]

In this year Henry VII. compromised his claim to the throne of France for 186,250*l.* besides 25,000 crowns yearly.

Sir William married a Mrs. Elizabeth Meggs, and resided in the parish of St.

---

[1] Fabyan's Chronicle.

[2] The arms given in Harl. MSS. 1049 and 1349, as well as by Heylyn, are Or, two bars gules, on the upper bar an escutcheon ermine.

Matthew Friday Street. He was buried in the church of St. Christopher by the Stocks.

THOMAS MIRFINE, Master 1515, son of George Mirfine of Ely, Cambridgeshire, Mayor A.D. 1518, temp. Henry VIII., Alderman of Bishopsgate Ward.

Arms: Or, on a chevron sable a mullet argent, a crescent for difference.

He married Alice, daughter of Oliver Squire, esquire, of Southby, county Hants, who was afterwards twice married; first to John Brigandine, Esquire, of Hants, and afterwards to Sir Edward North, of Kirtling or Catledge, county Cambridge. Thomas Mirfine was great-grandfather of Oliver Cromwell and John Hampden; his only daughter and heir was married to Sir Andrew Judde.[1] " He was buried in the north chancel of old St. Paul's together with Henry Barton, both of whom had fair tombs therein, with their tombs in alabaster, strongly coped with iron; all which, with the chapel, were pulled down in 1549 (3 Edward VI.) by the Duke of Somerset's appointment, and made use of for his building at Somerset House, in the Strand; the bones which lay in the vault underneath, amounting to more than a thousand cart-loads, being conveyed into Finnesbury Fields, and there laid on a moorish place, with so much soil to cover them as did raise the ground for three windmills to stand on, which have since been built there.[2]"

Sir JOHN CHAMPNEIS, son to Robert Champneis of Chew, in Somersetshire, Mayor A.D. 1534, temp. Henry VIII. Four times Master, A.D. 1527, 1528, 1530, and 1532.

Arms: Per pale argent and sable, within a bordure engrailed counterchanged a lion rampant gules.[3]

---

[1] See Harl. MSS. 1349.

[2] See Baker's North. i. 526. Dugdale's St. Paul's Cathedral, Ellis, p. 92.

[3] In Harl. MS. 1049 and 1349 the arms of Champneys or Champnies are thus blazoned: Per pale argent and sable, a lion rampant gules within a bordure engrailed counterchanged.

Sir ANDREW JUDDE, Mayor A.D. 1550, temp. Edward VI. Four times Master, A.D. 1538, 1544, 1551, 1555.

Arms: Gules, a fesse ragulé between three boar's heads couped close argent.[1]

Sir Andrew Judde, knight, the founder of Tonbridge School, was born at Tonbridge, but the date of his birth is not known. He was the youngest son of John Judde, Esq., and the nephew twice removed of Archbishop Chichele. An estate between Tonbridge and Tonbridge Wells belonged to his family, who as early as A.D. 1434 were reckoned one of the leading families of the county of Kent. From this property, which was situated on Quarry Hill and was called "Barden," the family removed to Ashford, near which also they had a seat, memorials of many of them being still in existence in the parish church of that place.[2]

Sir Andrew, when young, went to London, and was apprenticed to the Company of Skinners, a body at that time having considerable eminence in the metropolis as the chief, and probably the only, traders in skins and furs. It was by means of this trade that Sir Andrew amassed a large fortune, a considerable portion of which he so liberally expended on the foundation of Tonbridge school, and other trusts in connection with the Skinners' Company.

Sir Andrew is styled in old documents a "skinner and merchant of Muscovy," the latter being a title which in those days implied that he was a man of importance in the city of London.

Sir Andrew Judde himself took part in an expedition of the Merchants' Company, which used to transport their goods to the North of Russia in their own ships; and then, making use of boats shaped from the hollowed trunks of trees, towed them up the River Dwina to Vologda. From Vologda this merchandise was carried across country by a seven days' journey to Yaroslav, and thence transported

---

[1] Thus given in Harl. MSS. 1049, 1349. Quarterly, 1 and 4, Gules, a fess ragulé between three boar's heads couped close argent; 2 and 3, Azure, three lions rampant argent. The same authority says that "he was buried at St. Ellens in Bishopsgate Streete; he dwelled in the same howse that was Sir William Hollis, over agaynst Sir John Spencers; his only daughter Alice was married to Thomas Smyth, and was mother to Sir John, Sir Thomas, and Sir Richard Smyth now living."

[2] *History of Tonbridge School*, by S. Rivington.

down the Volga to Astrakhan, on the shores of the Caspian Sea. In this way, so early as the reign of Edward VI., English goods found their way into Persia and the remote regions of the East.

Sir Andrew Judde also visited the African coast and part of Guinea, and had brought home, at Edward VI.'s request, some gold dust for the use of the Royal Mint ; in fact, as the tablet to his memory says, " To Russia and Muscova, to Spayne and Gynny (Guinea), traveld He by land and sea."

In 1544 Sir Andrew Judde filled the office of Sheriff of London, and in 1550-1551 was Lord Mayor, during which time we have ample testimony, from " Proctour's History of Sir Thomas Wyatt's Rebellion," that Sir Andrew distinguished himself greatly by his loyalty. " Wyatt," says he, " and a fewe with him, went as farre as the drawebridge of Southwark, on the further side whereof he sawe the Lorde Admirall, the Lorde Maiour, Sir Andrew Judde, and one or two other, in consultation, for ordering of the bridge, where unto he gave diligent care a good tyme." These personal exertions in opposing Wyatt's rebellion helped him to gain the favour of Philip of Spain and of Queen Mary ; and during his mayoralty, which he kept in a house near St. Helen's church, Bishopsgate, he displayed great magnificence and hospitality. Sir Andrew was Lord Deputy and Mayor of the Staple of Calais, then in the hands of the English ; and in 1555, on September 4 in that year, he received Philip of Spain, who was on his way with a Royal retinue, including the Earls of Arundel, Pembroke, and Huntingdon, to visit the Emperor Charles V. at Brussels.

On this occasion Sir Andrew presented His Majesty with a purse containing a thousand marks in gold ; a magnificent gift from a private gentleman of that time. Philip was said to have been so gratified with this reception that he distributed a thousand crowns to the soldiers at Calais.

Sir Andrew Judde died on September 4, 1558, and was buried on the 14th, in St. Helen's Church, Bishopsgate, where a small tablet to his memory may be seen, affixed to the wall. On it is a figure of himself, kneeling, with a quaint inscription beneath.

The accompanying illustration is taken from a picture in the court-room at Skinners' Hall, and is traditionally supposed to be a portrait of Sir Andrew Judde.

Sir Andrew Judde.

Taken from his mural tablet in St. Helen's Church, Bishopsgate.

"To Russia and Muscova,
To Spayne and Gynny withoute fable
Traveld He by land and sea.
Both Mayre of London and staple,
The commonwealthe He norished
So worthelie in all his Daies,
That ech state fywell him loved,
To his perpetvale prayes.
Three wyves He had, one was Mary,
Fowre sons, one mayde, had he by her;
By Dame Mary had one Dowghtier.
Thus, in the month of September,
A thousand five hundred and fiftey
And eight, died this worthie staplar,
Worshipynge his posterytye."

Machyn (in his Diary, p. 174) mentions his funeral as having been conducted with great pomp and ceremony: "The xiv[th] day of September was buried Sir Andrew Jud, skinner, merchant of Muscovy, and late Mayor of London, with a pennon of armes and a x dozen of penselles, skocyons, and a herse of wax of v prynse pals, garnished with angelles, and poormen in new gownes, and Master Clarenshus (Clarencieux) King of Armes, and Master Somersett, harold, and the morrow masse and a sermon."[1]

His wives were:—

1. Mary, daughter of Sir Thomas Doon, Lord Mayor of London in 1519. By her he had four sons and one daughter. She died in 1550, and was buried in the church of St. Helen's on the 19th November in that year.

2. Annys.

3. Mary, heiress of Sir Thomas Mirfen, Lord Mayor of London in 1518, by whom he had one daughter, Alice; from her the family of the late Viscount Strangford is descended. This Alice Judde married Thomas Smythe, customer, *i.e.*, farmer of the public revenues, in the reigns of Queens Mary and Elizabeth, and father of Sir Thomas Smythe.

The Free Grammar School of Tonbridge, the native place of Sir Andrew Judde, was founded and endowed by him under letters

[1] *Londina Illustrata.*

patent of perpetuity, dated May 16th, 1553, the seventh year of Edward VI. He erected the school-house at the north end of the town, the original building being upwards of 100 feet in length; its front constructed in a plain, neat, and uniform style, with the sandstone of the vicinity. For the endowment of both his foundations he bought estates in the name of himself and Henry Fisher, who was afterwards his executor, and confided the management of those estates as well as of his school and almshouses to the Skinners' Company, of which he was a member.

After the decease of Sir Andrew Judde and Henry Fisher, to whom the property now described was originally conveyed, Andrew Fisher, the son of the latter, endeavoured to impeach the conveyances, and the whole affair was brought before the Parliament for examination. In the Journals of the House of Commons, 15th of Elizabeth, 1572, Monday, 30th June, appears an entry certifying to the House that the Right Hon. Sir Walter Mildmay, Chancellor, &c. and others, to whom had been committed the examination of a deed in the name of Henry Fisher, supposed to have been forged, "had found great untruth and impudence in the said Andrew Fisher; and that for very vehement presumptions they thought very evil of the deed; nevertheless, upon Fisher's submission, they had been contented to withdraw out of the Bill all words that touched him in infamy; and so the Bill penned passed this House with an assent on both sides, as well to help Tunbridge school as others that had bought land of the said Andrew's father bonâ fide."

At this time the Skinners' Company expended the sum of 4,000*l.* in prosecuting this and other suits; for Fisher again endeavoured to deprive both the school and Corporation of the property, under pretence that the latter was not rightly named in the Act of Foundation, which being again brought before the House of Commons upon the Company's petition, with Fisher's consent, another Act was passed, in 1588-89, the 31st of Elizabeth, confirming the former for the better assuring of the lands and tenements belonging to the free school of Tunbridge.[1]

The property thus given to the Skinners' Company to hold in trust for the school comprised some houses in Gracechurch Street valued at 30*l.* per annum, and about three acres of what was then pasture-

[1] Hasted's *History of Kent*, xi. 346, notes *x y.*

land, in the parish of St. Pancras. This was called the "Sandhills," and was bought by the founder for 346*l.* 6*s.* 8*d.* It is now covered with streets deriving their names from villages around Tonbridge, as Bidborough, Hadlow, Speldhurst, &c.

But Sir Andrew thought fit to execute a will as well as his previous charter. In this will, dated Sept. 2, 1558, he repeated his gift to the school, and added a further gift on different conditions. This consisted of a house in Old Swan Alley, one in St. Helen's, several in St. Mary Axe, and an annual rent-charge of ten pounds out of a messuage in Gracechurch Street.

The Wardens and Fellows of All Souls College, Oxford, are elected to act as moderators to the Governors from time to time. The stipend of the master is fixed at 20*l.* the usher at 8*l.* per annum. The master may elect or lodge not more than twelve, the usher not more than six scholars, and it is a singular fact that when Dr. Thomas Knox was examined before the Commissioners of Education in 1818 that the number of day scholars was only ten, and that of the boarders 32. There are now at present in the school about 230, less than one-half of whom are day-boys, and the rest are boarders either in the school-house under Dr. Welldon,[1] the present head master, or in the houses of the assistant-masters.

The exhibitions under the will of the founder are 16 in number, of 100*l.* each, four of which are given away every year; six of Sir Thomas Smith of 17*l.* per annum; four under the will of Sir James Lancaster; one under Mr. Edward Lewis's will of 15*l.*; and another by Mr. Henry Fisher, confined to Brazenose, Oxford, of 20*l.* per annum.

Sir Thomas White gave one of his fellowships at St. John's College, Oxford, for the benefit of scholars from this school.

Sir Andrew Judd also founded the almshouses in St. Helen's for six poor persons, freemen of the Company.

Sir Thomas Smythe, grandson of Sir Andrew Judde, was a great benefactor to the school. By his will, dated April 18, 1619, he bequeathed to the Skinners' Company houses in Old Change and in Lime Street, London, to dispose of their revenues according to his will. By

---

[1] Since the above was written the Rev. Canon Welldon, D.C.L. has resigned his position as Head Master of the School, and the Rev. Theo. B. Rowe, M.A. late Fellow of St. John's, Cambridge, third in First Classical Tripos, 31st Wrangler, and Chancellor's Medallist, has been elected Head Master by the Governors.

this means he was able to direct that the head master's salary should be increased by ten pounds, and the usher's by five pounds. He also founded six exhibitions of ten pounds per annum to last seven years, now increased to seventeen pounds each by accumulated amounts unapplied in former years through want of applicants, in aid of " the maintenance of six poor scholars at the universities who shall be most towardly and capable of learning, and who shall have been brought up and taught in the said school by the space of three years." During their university education these exhibitioners were to study divinity, and afterwards to enter the " sacred ministry." When ordained as clergymen they were required before and after their sermons to give thanks to God for His mercy toward them in the contribution of their benefactor for their maintenance, for the reason that it should excite others to do good and charitable works.

HEAD MASTERS OF THE SCHOOL FROM THE FOUNDATION TO THE PRESENT TIME.

A.D.
1558 to 1578. Rev. John Proctor, M.A.
1578 ,, 1588. Rev. John Stockwood, M.A.
1588 ,, . Rev. William Hatch, M.A.
 ,, 1640. Rev. Michael Jenkins, M.A.
1640 ,, 1647. Rev. Thomas Horne, D.D.
1647 ,, 1657. Rev. Nicholas Grey, D.D.
1657 ,, 1661. Rev. John Goad, B.D.
1661 ,, 1680. Rev. Christopher Wase, B.D.
1680 ,, 1714. Rev. Thomas Roots, M.A.
1714 ,, 1743. Rev. Richard Spencer, M.A.[1]
1743 ,, 1761. Rev. James Cawthorn, M.A.
1761 ,, 1770. Rev. Johnson Towers, M.A.
1770 ,, 1778. Rev. Vicesimus Knox, LL.B.
1778 ,, 1812. Rev. Vicesimus Knox, D.D.
1812 ,, 1843. Rev. Thomas Knox, D.D.
1843 ,, 1875. Rev. James Ind Welldon, D.C.L.[2]
1875 Rev. Theo. B. Rowe, M.A.

[1] P. 21.
[2] By the Court Books, A.D. 1672, it would appear that the Skinners when applied to appointed one of the ushers at Tonbridge to the head-mastership of Kingston, Southampton.

Sir RICHARD DOBBES, 5 Edward VI., son of Robert Dobbes of Bailby, Yorkshire; Sheriff 1543; Alderman of Tower Ward; Mayor 1551. Master, A.D. 1542, 1543, 1548, 1550, 1554. Buried at St. Margaret Moyses, Bread Street.

Arms: Per pale argent and sable, a chevron engrailed between three unicorn's heads erased and counterchanged.[1]

There is a portrait of Sir Richard Dobbs, knt. in the court-room of Christ's Hospital, ætatis suæ 65. He is habited in his robes of office, and wears a venerable beard, a small black hat, and has a plaited frill round his neck; he holds a book in his right hand with the forefinger in the leaves, and under the picture are the following lines:

"Christ's Hospital erected was a passinge deed of pittee,
What time Sir Richard Dobbs was Mair of this most fam's Citee;
Who carefull was in Government and furthered moche the same;
Also a benefactor good and joyed to see its frame.
Whoes portraiture heare his frends have sett to putt eache wight in minde
To imitate his virtuous deeds as God hath us assigned."

Londinium Redivivum.

I cannot do better than sum up the deeds of this worthy man by quoting from Bishop Ridley's letter[2] shortly before his martyrdom to his friend Sir George Barnes:

"O Dobbs, Dobbs, Alderman and Knight, thou in thy yeare did win my heart for evermore for thine honorable act, that most blessed work of God, of the erection and setting up of Christ's Holy Hospitals and truly religious houses, which by thee and through thee were begun, for thou, like a man of God, when the matter was moved for Christ's poore silly members to be holpen from extreme misery, and hunger, and famine; thy hearte I saye was mooved with pity, and, as Christ's high honorable officer in that cause, thou calledst together thy bretheren the Aldermen of the City, before whom thou breakest the matter for the poore; thou didst plead their cause, yea and not only with thine owne person didst set forth Christ's cause, but to further the matter thou broughtest me into the

---

[1] According to Harl. MSS. 1049 and 1349, and also in Heylyn: Per pale argent and sable, a chevron engrailed between three unicorn's heads erased, each charged with three guttées, all counterchanged. "Buried at St. Margaret Moyses in Friday Streete, where he dwelled in the howse that was lately Roger Clarks, sometime Sheriff and Alderman of London."

[2] Stowe, p. 176.

THE COMPANY OF SKINNERS. 55

Council Chamber of the City, before the Aldermen alone, whom thou hadst assembled there to hear me, and to speak what I could say as an advocate by office and duty in the poore man's cause. The Lord wrought with thee and gave thee the consent of thy brethren, whereby the matter was brought to the Common Council, and so to the whole body of the City; by whom with an uniform consent it was committed to be drawn, ordered, and devised by a certain number of the most witty Citizens and politick, endued also with godliness and with ready hearts to set forward such a noble act, as could be chosen in all the whole City; and thy like true and faithful Minister, both to the City and their master Christ, so ordered, devised, and brought the matter forth, that thousands of poore silly members of Christ, that else for extreme hunger, and misery, should have famished and perished, that be relieved, holpen, and brought up, and shall have cause to bless the Aldermen of that time, the Common Council, and the whole body of the City, but especially thee, O Dobbs, and those chosen men by whom this honorable work was begun and wrought." [1]

We are indebted to Henry Machyn, Merchant Taylor, for the following description in his Diary [2] of his funeral, which appears to have been celebrated with all civic honours, A.D. 1555.

The xviij day of May at after-non was bered ser Recherd Dobes latt mayre of London and altherman; ther wher at ys berehyng mony worshefull men ;......... my lord mare and the swordbeyrer in blake, and the recorder cheyff morner, and master Eggyllfield and master (*blank*) and master .... [ov]erscar, and a lx mornars, and ij haroldes of armes, and the althermen and the shreyffes, and master Chestur bare ys cott armur, [with] helmett and targatt, sword, a standard, and penone, and iiij baneres [of] images, and a xxx pore men in rosett gownes holdyng .... torches, and iiij gylt chandyllstykes with iiij grett tapurs [with] armes on them; and all the cherche and the stret hangyd with blake, and the qwyre, and armes, and ij grett whyt branchys; and alle the masturs of the hospetalle boyth althermen and the commenas with ther gren stayffes in ther handes; and the chyeff of the hospetalle, and prestes and clarkes; and after *dirige* to the place to drynke; and the morow masse of *requiem* ij masses, on of the Trenete in pryke songe, and a-nodur of our Lade; and after a sermon, and after to dener: and ther wher x dosen of skochyons.[3]

[The ...... day was the funeral of lady Dobbes, late the] wyff of ser Recherd Dobes knyght and skynner late mayre, with a harold of armes, and she had a pennon of armes and iiij dosen and d' skochyons; [she was buried] in the parryche of sant Margat Moyses in Fryday stret; [she] gayff xx good blake gownes to xx powre women; she gayffe xl blake gownes to men and women; [master] Recherdsun mad the sermon, and the clarkes syngyng, [and] a dolle of money of xx nobulles, and a grett dener after, and the compene of the Skynners in ther leverey.

---

[1] Stowe, i. 176. Rev. W. Trollope, Christ's Hospital, p. 342.

[2] Machyn's Diary, p. 106.

[3] Heraldic ensigns of the lowest order.

Sir Wolstan Dixie was the youngest son of Thos. Dixie of Catworth, Huntingdonshire, Mayor A.D. 1585, temp. 27 Eliz. Master, A.D. 1573, 1576, 1580, 1588, 1592.

Arms: Azure, a lion rampant or, a chief of the last.

During his mayoralty there appears to have been a great muster of the citizens both by reason of domestic insurrection and to resist the then contemplated Spanish Invasion; large contributions were raised by the citizens, towards which fund Sir Wolstan Dixie gave 1,000*l.* for which the Queen paid 10 per cent. About this time she found it better to borrow from her own subjects than negotiate with foreign merchants. We find that in the year 1588 the members of the twelve Livery Companies raised a sum amounting to no less than 51,000*l.* Shortly after which, the Queen being at Greenwich, the City Militia was mustered before her, for six or eight days lying intrenched about Blackheath, to the number of between 4,000 or 5,000 men; amongst these we find the Skinners furnished 174 men, fully equipped, and contributed a sum of 163*l.* 5*s.* He married, firstly, his master's daughter, Walkenden, secondly, Agnes, daughter of Sir Christopher Draper. Agnes was the founder of a Greek and Hebrew lectureship at Emanuel College. He died without issue at the age of 69, and was buried in St. Michael's Bassishaw in 1593. "He dwelled in the howse," says the MS., "where Sir Leonard Halyday now dwelleth," and like Sir Andrew Judd amassed a large fortune as a Russia merchant.

There is an excellent portrait of him in the court-room of Christ's Hospital as president in 1592, of which foundation he was a liberal benefactor, as appears on a shield in the corner. The knight is habited in his Lord Mayor's dress; his features show considerable firmness of character as he leans on a table holding a richly embroidered glove in his right hand; he wears a venerable beard, and hat of the period.[1]

Besides assisting liberally in the building of Peterhouse, Cambridge, he left in trust to the Skinners' Company a sum of 700*l.* towards founding a grammar-school at Market Bosworth, Leicestershire. The

---

[1] Stowe, i. 37.

Skinners, however, appear to have been averse to accepting the trust, no doubt on account of the annoyance and loss they had sustained in resisting the claims of Andrew Fisher to the property devised by him for a similar purpose in the foundation of Tonbridge School,[1] in the prosecution of which trust some 4,000*l.* are stated to have been swallowed up.

A complaint was therefore entered in the Court of Chancery by Wolstan Dixie, a nephew of the testator, and an order was obtained, A.D. 1600,[2] that the bequest and the trust accompanying it should be transferred to him; and statutes were by his direction drawn up for the government of the school.

To Christ's Hospital he gave yearly for ever 42*l.*

To Emanuel College, Cambridge, the maintenance of two Fellows and two Scholars, 600*l.*

To the building of the College 50*l.*

To be lent unto poor merchants 500*l.* thrifty young men free of the Company.

For marriage portions to poor maids 100*l.*

To poor strangers, Dutch and French, 50*l.*

Sir STEPHEN SLANEY, or SLANY, son of John Slaney of Mitton, in Staffordshire, A.D. 1595, 37 Eliz. Master, A.D. 1585, 1591, 1598.

Arms: Gules, a bend between three martlets or.

Alderman of Portsoken Ward and President of Christ's Hospital.

He married Margaret, the daughter of Jasper Pheasant, and had five sons and six daughters.

There appears to have been a great scarcity of corn during his mayoralty, and orders were issued by the Privy Council for remedying the dearth, when one Delaney printed and published a ballad or dialogue ridiculing these orders and endeavouring to stir up disaffection to the existing government, for which offence Sir Stephen Slaney committed him to the Compter.[3]

---

[1] Rivington's *Tonbridge*, p. 46.
[2] Lond. and Mid. Trans. ii. 25-36.   [3] Stowe, i. 442.

Sir Stephen Slaney was buried at St. Stephen's, Walbrook, 1608.[1]

Sir RICHARD SALTONSTALL, Master, A.D. 1589, 1593, 1595, 1599, returned as Member for the City 28 Elizabeth, Mayor 1597.

Arms: Or, a bend between two eagles displayed sable.

He was the second son of Sir Gilbert Saltonstall, of Halifax, Yorkshire, and resided at Okendon, in the county of Essex. He married Susan, the only daughter of Thomas Poyntz, of North Okendon, co. Essex, by whom he had two sons, Sir Richard and Sir Samuel Saltonstall.[2] His granddaughter Anne married John Hurly, Skinner and Merchant Adventurer. His great-granddaughter, an heiress, born 5 April, 1711, married the Honourable George Montague, afterwards 2nd Earl of Halifax, K.B. from whom descended Francis North, first Earl of Guildford. Sir R. Saltonstall appears to have purchased the manor and advowson of Chipping Warden, in the county of Northampton, some time prior to 1619, of Edward Griffin, esq.[3] His arms were on a panel at No. 76, High Street, Aldgate, where he resided, and are given by Mr. J. G. Smithers in vol. i. of the London and Middlesex Society's Transactions, p. 375.

The Parliamentary Commissioners in 1655 certified the parsonage as having a representative worth of 88l. per annum, in the patronage of Richard Saltonstall, esq.; at this time Richard Stanwick was incumbent. The manor house, standing on the east side of the church, was erected by the Saltonstalls in the seventeenth century. Saltonstall was also a Merchant Adventurer.

In a letter written by him to Lord Burghley he says that he had used all diligence as became him, and called the Merchant Adventurers together, and that they had agreed to furnish the 3,320l. 8s. required by Lord Burghley, of which 2,000l. was for a month's pay of the army in Picardy.[4]

---

[1] In Harl. MS. 1349 he is said to have died on the 28 December, 1608, and to have been buried at St. Swithyn's by London Stone on the 31 January following.

[2] Baker's *Northampton*, i. 526.

[3] Ibid. p. 528.   [4] Domestic State Papers, pp. 361, 374.

Sir WILLIAM COKAYNE, Mayor 1619, Alderman of Castle Baynard Ward, and first Governor of the Irish Society. Master, A.D. 1625, 1640.

Arms: Argent, three cocks gules, armed and legged sable.

Sir William Cokayne was second son of William Cokayne of Baddesley Ensor, co. Warwick, Citizen and Skinner of London, (by Elizabeth, daughter of Roger Medcalfe, of Wensleydale, co. York, and of Alspade and Meriden, co. Warwick, also Citizen and Skinner of London,) and grandson of Roger Cokayne, of Sturson, in the parish of Ashbourne, co. Derby, which Roger was younger son of William, second son of Sir John Cokayne, knt. of Ashbourne, by Isabel, daughter of Sir Hugh Shirley, knt. He was born 1560, admitted free of the Company of Skinners by patrimony 28 March, 1590, was a Merchant of London, Alderman and Lord Mayor as aforesaid, and was knighted at his own residence, Cokayne House, in Broad Street, London (afterwards the site of the Old South Sea House and now of the City of London Club), on 8 June, 1616, after having entertained the King and the Prince of Wales at a banquet. Purchased the manor and estate of Rushton, co. Northampton, of Elmesthorpe, Swepston, and Nethercote, co. Leicester, of Coombe Nevill, in Kingston, co. Surrey, &c. He married 22 June, 1596, at St. Leonard's, Eastcheap, Mary, youngest daughter of Richard Morris, sometime master of the Ironmongers' Company, by Maud, daughter of John Daborne, of Guildford, Surrey, sometime mayor of that town. Sir William died 20 October, 1626, aged 66, at Coombe Nevill, and was buried in great state in St. Paul's Cathedral, where a handsome monument was erected to him, engraved in Dugdale's History of St. Paul's.[1] His widow remarried, 6 July, 1630,

---

[1] Dugdale has fortunately rescued his monument from oblivion; it stood in the south-west part of the choir of old St. Paul's. He and his wife are represented as recumbent figures, lying on a sarcophagus, with four daughters kneeling in front of it, while at the head of Sir William two other daughters are represented kneeling, and at his feet his son Charles, besides two babies in swaddling clothes under the one side, and two children (who died in his lifetime) kneeling under the other. The inscription was as follows:—

Gulielmus Cokainus Eques auratus, civis et senator Londinensis, septemq. abhinc annis urbis præfectus: antiqua Cokainorum Derbiensium familia oriundus:

at St. Peter le Poor, Henry Carey, Lord Hunsdon, first Earl of Dover. She died 24 December, 1618, and was buried with her first husband.

Of Sir William's children, besides several who died young, Charles Cokayne, only surviving son and heir, was created 11 Aug. 1642 Viscount and Baron Cullen in the peerage of Ireland, with a special remainder, failing the heirs male of his body (which happened 11 Aug. 1810) to the younger sons of his sister Martha, Dowager Countess of Holderness, by her then husband Montague Bertie, Lord Willoughby d'Eresby (afterwards second Earl of Lindsey), in right of which the present Earl of Lindsey is entitled to the Viscountcy of Cullen.

1. Mary, married 22 April, 1620, at St. Peter's aforesaid, Charles Howard, Lord Howard of Effingham, second Earl of Nottingham, and died s.p. 6 February, 1650-1.

2. Ann, married Sir Hatton Fermor, of Easton Neston, co. Northampton, knt. by whom she was ancestress of the Lords Lempster and Earls of Pomfret. She died 17 May, 1668.

3. Martha, married firstly, John Ramsay, Earl of Holdernesse in Scotland, and secondly Mountague Bertie, Lord Willoughby d'Eresby, afterwards (1642) Earl of Lindsey and K.G. By him she was ancestress of the Dukes of Ancaster and of the present Earls of Lindsey, Lords Willoughby d'Eresby, Dukes of Leeds, &c. She died July 1641.

qui bono publico vixit, et damno publico decessit; et gaudio publico Regem Jacobum ad decorem hujus Domus Dei senescentis jam et corrugatæ restituendum, solenniter huc venientem, Consulatu suo magnifice excepit: idcirco in Templo publico, ad æternam rei memoriam hic situs est. At vero et Famæ celebritas, quæ vigit in ore hominum, et gloria beatitudinis, quam migrando adeptus est, et splendor sobolis quam numerosam genuit, atq. nobilem reliquit, junctim efficiunt omnia, ne dicatur hic situs est.

Una cum illo tot homines mortui, quot in illo defunctæ sunt virtutes; simulq. et acies ingenii et popularis eloquii suada, et morum gravitas, et probitas vitæ, et candor mentis, et animi constantia, et prudentia singularis, et veri Senatoris insignia hic sepulta sunt.

Jam tuum est, Lector, fœlicitatis ad culmen anhelare per ista vestigia laudis, et venerandi imitatione exempli curare, ne unquam virtutis sic semina intereant, ut dicatur hic sepulta sunt.

Obiit xx Octob. An. Dom. 1626.
Et Ætatis suæ LXVI.

Detached Corinthian columns in Ante (with a low semi-arch between them carrying the inscription) support a pediment; on the entablature appear sculptured the family arms, viz.: 1, Cokayne; 2, Herthull; 3, Deyville; 4, Savage; 5, Rossington; 6, Edensor; and 7, "Arg. three stags sable."

Standing on scrolls on the pediment are four statues, and in the centre the

4. Elizabeth, married Thomas Fanshawe, first Viscount Fanshawe in the peerage of Ireland, and was ancestress of the succeeding viscounts. She died February 1667-8.

5. Abigail, married John Carey, Viscount Rochford, Earl of Dover, son of Henry, first Earl of Dover above-named, by his first wife. She died February 1687-8.

6. Jane, married the Hon. James Sheffield, younger son of Edmund, Earl of Mulgrave, K.G. She died September 1683.

In 1620 we find Sir Thomas Smith, Sir Thomas Lowe, and Sir William Cokayne,[1] appointed by an order of Council on a commission for settling all difference between the Spanish and Turkey merchants, who were required to take up certain loans and to furnish their quota to the expedition against the pirates in the narrow seas, and to "prepare good and serviceable ships, furnished with able men and wholesome provisions in proportion to the tonnage employed by the King's ships," for which they were to be reimbursed by levies of one per cent. on all imports and exports.[2]

This, however, was not the only way in which he lent his services for the use of the State. When the East India and Muscovy Companies[3] were unable to meet their liabilities, Sir William Cokayne, in conjunction with Sir Baptist Hicks and Peter Vanlore, advanced them a sum of no less than 30,000*l.*, for the reimbursement of which an order of Council was passed for repayment from the first moneys that came in upon the credit of the Palatine, the Council to enter into bonds with the said knights for security.[4] In conjunction with Sir John Catcher and Abraham Cartwright Sir William Cokayne was fortunate enough to obtain a grant from the Crown of a monopoly to transport and dispose of all tin in the counties of Devon and Cornwall for a period of seven years.

shield and crest; on either side are two recesses with Corinthian pilasters and half-circular pediments.

Besides the great coat of seven quarterings mentioned above, the arms of Lady Cokayne (viz., "Vert, a stag or," being the coat of Morris) appear twice on the tomb impaled with Cokayne; and there are shields over each of the six daughters and over the one son, *i.e.* the seven surviving children. The shield over the latter had the arms of Cokayne impaling O'Brien (Earls of Thomond), while those over the two daughters (above) contained (1) Howard, Earl of Nottingham, impaling Cokayne; (2) Ramsay, Earl of Holdernesse, impaling Cokayne. Three of the four shields over the four daughters below contained a blank space impaling Cokayne, while the fourth contained Fermor impaling Cokayne.

[1] Domestic State Papers, 1620, p. 298. [2] Ibid. 1621, p. 308.
[3] Ibid. 10. [4] Domestic State Papers, 1620.

He was also one of the first members of the Irish Society appointed by the City for colonizing Londonderry.[1]

We find him also occupying the position of President of St. Thomas's Hospital,[2] as well as a benefactor and a governor of Christ's Hospital. There is in the court-room of this last-mentioned excellent charity a good portrait of him with a venerable beard, his eyes and mouth expressive of decision and firmness of purpose.

(For description of pageant see page 39.)

Sir RICHARD DEAN, Mayor 1628. He was son of George Dean of Dunmow in Essex. Alderman of Candlewick. Master 1609.

Arms: Argent, on a chevron sable, between three Cornish choughs proper, as many cross-crosslets or.[3]

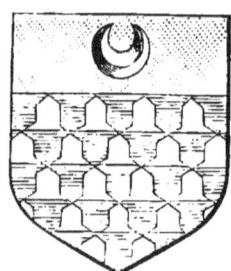

ROBERT TITCHBORNE, or TICHBORN, son of John Titchborne of Cowden, in Kent, Mayor, A.D. 1657. Master, A.D. 1650.

Arms: Vair, a on chief or a crescent.

Sir Robert Tichborn appears to have been a descendant of a branch of the Tichborns of Hants, who were created barons[4] temp. Henry II. His father lived in an old manor-house called Creppenden, about five miles from Edenbridge; some portion of it still remains and is now a farmhouse. In one of the rooms there is a fine carved oak chimney-piece with this inscription carved on it in bold relief:—

When we are dead
And laid in grave
And all our bones are rotten,
By this shall we
Remembered be
Or else we were forgotten.
R. and D. T. 1607.

Richard and Dorothy Tichborn.

---

[1] Court Books. [2] Domestic State Papers, p. 546.
[3] In Heylyn's *Help to English History*, 1773, the arms are given as Argent, on a chevron gules between three Cornish choughs proper, as many crosses patée or.
[4] Berry's *County Peerage of Hants;* Stowe, ii. 146.

The family successfully carried on one of the iron-foundries which at that time were confined chiefly to Kent and Sussex; and from the foundry here established the Parliamentary forces were assisted with a supply of ordnance.[1]

Living at a time when the struggle between Charles I. and the nation was becoming every day more bitter, the arbitrary acts of the King would recall to his mind those of Elizabeth, and the death of his kinsman [2] Chidiock Tichborn, who for his part in the Babington conspiracy was executed on Tower Hill. Added to this, accounts would reach him publicly if not privately from his relative Sir Henry Tichborn (who was at the siege of Drogheda) of the circumstances of mismanagement and cruelty which added to that unfortunate rebellion. Occupying as he did an honourable position amongst his fellow citizens, he would also be alarmed at the threatening attitude of the King, who by placing troops in the Tower [3] endeavoured to overawe the Londoners. Swayed by these and such like considerations we must not be surprised to find that he threw in his lot with the Parliamentary forces at that time struggling for the mastery; and, taking the rank and title of Colonel, was appointed Lieutenant of the Tower, on the retirement of Sir Isaac Pennington, by General Fairfax then Chief Constable, as well for services rendered in the Kentish rising as for his influence in the City. While occupying this post, A.D. 1648,[4] Thomas Adams, John Langham, and James Brue, Aldermen of London, were committed to his custody. Finding that they were likely to be carried before the Lords Justices, they addressed a petition both to their honoured friend Colonel Tichborn and also to the lords assembled in Parliament, protesting against the illegality of the proceeding, and the fine of 500*l*. which had been imposed upon them, alleging weighty reasons and concluding thus:

Your Petitioners, being Free Commoners of England, according to the known laws of the land (de jure) claim their birthright, which is to be tried by God and their country, in his Majesties Court of Justice, by the sworn judges of the law, and a jury of their equals, of their own neighbourhood, where the pretended fact was done, the courts of justice being open.

---

[1] A specimen may be seen on the lawn in front of the Rev. J. Hervey's house, Cowden, with the name of Tichborn on it.
[2] Bailey's *Tower of London*, ii. 507.   [3] Ibid. p. 97.
[4] Stowe, ii. 300.

While holding this post, hope was entertained of restoring tranquillity, and negotiations were entered into between Cromwell and the King (who was then a prisoner in the Isle of Wight). Amongst other conditions it was required that the government of the Tower of London should be confided to the city for ten years. In the following year Fairfax resigned, and Cromwell appointed Sir John Berkshot to succeed him. General insurrection appears now to have broken out in various parts of the country, amongst others at Tonbridge and Redhill.[1] The Council of State being apprised thereof, a party of horse were sent to the place of rendezvous, when some prisoners were taken, and the rest dispersed.

In these and other matters Tichborne had no doubt rendered valuable service to his party, and we find his name subsequently appearing amongst the leading members of the House of Commons, who were appointed a High Court of Justice, for the trying and judging of Charles Stuart, King of England, Die Sabbati, January 6, 1648.

The Court met in the Painted Chamber at Westminster on the following day, and on the 12th of January Tichborne, Col. Blackstone, and Fry, all members of the Court, were appointed to make preparations for the trial of the King : "That it should be performed in a solemn manner, and that they take care for other necessary provision and accommodation in and about the trial, and appoint and command such workmen in and to their assistance as they think fit."[2] On another occasion his name appears on a Committee for considering the circumstances and order of the trial, together with Sir Hardress Waller, Col. Whalley, Mr. Scott, Col. Harrison, and others. Twice only was he absent, although the Court sat twelve times in the Painted Chamber and five times at Whitehall; on the last occasion his name appears as one of those who signed the fatal warrant of Jan. 27th.

In 1650 he and Sir Richard Chiverton (both Skinners) were elected to serve the office of sheriff, and it is in this year that his name appears in the Court Books as Master of the Company. He was afterwards, on the feast of St. Michael, 1656, elected Mayor, Sir Anthony Bateman, a Skinner, being one of his sheriffs.

[1] Heath's *History of the Civil War*.

[2] Copy of Journal of High Court of Justice for Trial of King Charles I., by Neilson, LL.D., 1683.

The year 1660 brought changes and troubles to Tichborne. The apprentices of the City[1] assembled by thousands and clamoured for a free Parliament; people everywhere refused to pay taxes. General Monk was advancing towards London, and he had no sooner declared himself in favour of a free Parliament than the prospect of a restoration was hailed with delight. At a Court[2] held at Skinners' Hall the 29th day of March, it was resolved that the Council of State should be invited, and a Committee was chosen to dispose all matters and things thereunto belonging, and to appoint a day for the feast with his Excellency, to which purpose the Master and Wardens, our Lord Tichborne, Sir R. Chiverton, Alderman Bonar, Mr. Rogers, Mr. Burdett, Mr. Bateman, Mr. Bowles, Mr. Joliffe, Mr. Dawson, Mr. Alsopp, Mr. Albin, Mr. Corbill, and Mr. Lewis the younger, were appointed; to these, six other names were afterwards added; amongst these latter we find that of Sir William Cokayne. The entertainment took place on the 4th of April, when a panegyric was spoken in honour of his Excellency, who was called the Deliverer.[3]

On the 7th of May following a precept from the Lord Mayor and Common Council was read at the Court requiring the Company to advance and pay into the Chamber 504*l.* to help make up a sum of 12,000*l.* for the King's most Excellent Majesty as a present; 10,000*l.* for him and 2,000*l.* for the two Dukes; wherewith the Company, though willing enough for the work, were displeased with the word " require," considering it in the nature of a demand, whereunto it was answered that it was an error of the Clerk of Common Council, and not the intent of the Court, and that it should be amended, and " desired " be inserted, whereupon the money was advanced.

On the 21st a further precept was received, requiring the Company to be in readiness with twenty-four of the most comely and graceful persons of the Company, every one of them to be well horsed, and well arrayed with velvet plush or satin, and chains of gold; to be waited upon by a footman in advance, to attend on the King's Majesty, if he shall happen upon his happy return from beyond the sea to pass through the City of London, thereby to manifest the Company's affection and duty to his Highness, and to have all rails, banners, and ornaments ready.

[1] Macaulay, i. 145.   [2] Court Books.
[3] The address was printed, but the copy at Skinners' Hall cannot now be found.

Sir R. Tichborne was at this time beyond the sea, where he had no doubt fled, possibly to sue for pardon, relying on the clemency of the King and his proclamation of amnesty.[1] His success may be inferred from a proclamation signed by Charles, dated Breda, Oct. 9th, wherein Owen Roe, Augustus Garland, and R. Titchborne, are described as " having been guilty of the most detestable and bloody treason, in sitting upon and giving judgment upon the life of our royal father, and have fled and obscured themselves." They were required to surrender themselves to the Speaker within fourteen days, under pain of being exempt from pardon and indemnity, both with respect to their lives and estates. Relying, no doubt, on the favour of his friend General Monk, he and the others surrendered, and were committed to the care of Sir John Robinson, his Majesty's Lieutenant of the Tower. A Special Commission of thirty-eight members was appointed to take charge of the trial of the Regicides, which commenced its sittings at Hicks's Hall, Oct. 6th, amongst whom we find General Monk, now Duke of Albemarle, and others, who unblushingly consented to try their comrades for fidelity to the cause which they themselves had betrayed. Twenty-nine persons were remanded for trial at the Sessions House in the Old Bailey. The trial commenced Oct. 10th and lasted eight days. Tichborne pleaded not guilty to the manner and form of the indictment, and when called upon for his defence alleged his early age, and ignorance when he sat with the Commission upon the King; that he had not acted with malice, and, had he known what he then knew, he would as soon have gone into a fiery oven as the Commission, concluding with these words : " My Lords, I came in on the proclamation, and now 1 am here. I have in truth given your Lordships a clear and full account. Whatever the law shall pronounce because I am ignorant, I hope there will be room found for that mercy and grace that was I think intended by the proclamation, and I hope by the Parliament of England." To which the Council replied : " We shall give no evidence against the prisoner ; he said he did it ignorantly, and I hope and do believe he is penitent, and as far as Parliament thinks fit to show mercy I shall be very glad."

All the prisoners were convicted, and the Lord Chief Baron pronounced sentence accordingly. Of the twenty-nine tried, ten only suffered the extreme penalty of the law, and Tichborne's name does

[1] State Trials, v. 1002 to 1230.

not appear amongst them. Although he was fortunate enough to escape from paying the extreme penalty of the law, his property was nevertheless sequestered, as the following extract from the State Papers shows:—

"In June 1660 a warrant issued commanding Sir R. Mauleverer to search for the plate and jewels of Alderman Tichborne, said to be immured in his late dwelling-house, Noble Street, London, and to take a catalogue thereof."[1]

"A petition was also presented by Catherine, wife of Paul Feryn, groom of the robes, for the lease of Old Court Manor, part of the manor of East Greenwich, forfeited by his attainder, together with the parsonage, ballast wharf, &c., at a rent of 6l. 13s. 4d., in lieu of a debt of 2,000l. due to her father's husband for perfumes supplied to the late King and Queen."[2]

In an order of Common Council,[3] Sept. 27th, 1660, the Lord Mayor is ordered forthwith to repair unto the Ward of Farringdon for nomination in place of Master Alderman Titchborne, who is disabled by a proviso in the late Act of Oblivion, whereby all those who signed on the 5th of December, 1648, and did give sentence of death upon any person in the late illegal High Court of Justice, or signed the warrant of any person therein condemned, are made incapable of bearing office.

In 1661 a grant of his stock and other moneys in the East India Company was made to Sir Henry Littleton, Bart.[4]

In a subsequent grant to the Duke of York of all arrears of rent arising out of the estates of all persons attainted of high treason for the horrid murder of the late King, those of Carew and Robert Titchborne are excepted, having as we have seen been elsewhere appropriated.

Our portrait of Sir Robert is copied from an interesting print in the possession of the Corporation of London. It has been stated that he was the last Lord Mayor who rode on horseback to Westminster, but this is inaccurate; Sir William Heathcote, knight and baronet, proceeded in this way when elected to the Mayoralty in the year 1710.

Strype (p. 121) mentions an old timber building, existing in 1716, at the upper end of Fitches Court, Aldersgate, as being the house wherein he lived; the house escaped in the Fire of London when all others around were consumed.

[1] Domestic State Papers, Charles II.
[2] Ibid. p. 344.
[3] Guildhall Report, 67, fol. 136.
[4] Ibid. Docquet Book, p. 101.

Sir RICHARD CHIVERTON, son of Henry Chiverton of Trehouse in Cornwall, Mayor A.D. 1658.

Knighted by Cromwell 1653 and by Charles II. 1663.

ARMS: Argent, on a mount vert a tower triple-towered sable.

Sir ANTHONY BATEMAN, Mayor A.D. 1664, son of Robert Bateman, Chamberlain of London A.D. 1633, and one of the representatives in Parliament for the City;

Arms: Or, three crescents, each surmounted with a star gules.

He was appointed one of the commissioners for convening a free Parliament for the city on the entry of General Monk.

(For description of pageant see page 40.)

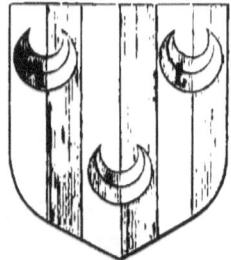

Sir GEORGE WATERMAN, son of John Waterman, Mayor A.D. 1674, a vintner at the King's Arms, Southwark; he lived at the Helmet in Thames Street. M.P. for Westminster. His daughter married Judge Jeffries.

Arms: Paly of six argent and gules, three crescents counterchanged.

(For description of pageant see page 40.)

Sir THOMAS PILKINGTON, son of Sir Thomas Pilkington, son of John Pilkington of Okeham, was descended from a good Northamptonshire family. He was thrice Master of the Company, in 1677, 1681, and 1682, and three times Lord Mayor of London, viz., in 1689, 1690, 1691.[1]

The accompanying photograph has been taken from the portrait of Sir Thomas which hangs on the staircase.

Arms: Argent, a cross patonce, **voided** gules.

[1] Stowe, p. 151.

He was elected as Member of Parliament for the City of London 1680, and again in 1689. He appears to have lived in times of great political excitement, and to have been violently opposed to the Court party in the latter part of the reign of Charles II., when, as Macaulay tells us,[1]

The Habeas Corpus Act was suspended, and the Presbyterians of Scotland were suffering under a tyranny such as England in the worst times had never known ; when the whole nation under the Whigs were ripe for insurrection, and the unscrupulous and hot-headed chiefs of the party formed and discussed schemes of resistance, and were heard, if not with approbation, yet with the show of acquiescence by better men than themselves.

It was at such a time (1671) that Pilkington was elected sheriff. Not long after we find him on the occasion of the King's return from Newmarket, and that of his brother the Duke of York from Scotland, expressing his opinion somewhat too freely, for which he was accused and prosecuted by the Duke of York for *scandalum magnatum*, because at a meeting of the Court of Aldermen Sir Henry Tulse and Sir William Hooker swore to his having used the words, " He hath burnt the city and is now come to cut the people's throats;"[2] for this he was prosecuted, and the case tried at Hertford. Mr. Pilkington made very little defence, and the jury after a short interval found for the plaintiff, damages 100,000*l*.; a sentence, as Macaulay observes, "tantamount to perpetual imprisonment," although the execution of it was for some cause or other deferred. The severity of the sentence however does not appear to have damped his ardour for the Protestant cause, and we next hear of him taking a prominent part in the election for sheriff A.D. 1683.

From time immemorial the Lord Mayor had exercised the privilege of nominating one sheriff, by drinking to him at the Bridge House feast, the Livery electing the other.[3] This custom the Lord Mayor determined, as it had fallen somewhat into disuse, to revive and to exercise, and was backed by the power and influence of the Court party.

At this time there appear to have been two parties, of whom Sir John Moore, the Mayor, sided with the Court, while the others were continually meeting at coffee-houses and raving about the state of affairs, using the cries of " Popery," " French," and " arbitrary power " frequently.

[1] Macaulay, i. 267. [2] Cobbett's *State Trials*, ix. 194.
[3] Stowe, i. 353.

The difficulty was, however, to find some one to stand for sheriff who would not fine off; the opposite party denounced all who were inclined to do so, and "hanging," "knocking out of brains," "hell and damnation" (if they might presume so far), was to be the fate of those who might stand. While this was going on, my Lord Mayor according to custom sent the cup to Mr. North, afterwards Sir Dudley North, who was not at the Bridge House feast. The opposite party desired the election of Papillon and Dubois. On the day of the election the dispute ran so high that curses and threats were used at the Common Hall, and as the Court of Aldermen could not agree the Lord Mayor desired to adjourn; this was disputed, but after much clamour an adjournment was made, and Sir John Moore left the chair. Pilkington and Shute with the liverymen of their party thought fit not to obey the adjournment, and held on the Common Hall, and afterwards proceeded to election by setting up a poll, and elected Papillon and Dubois. The illegality of the act is obvious, and warrants were immediately issued by the King in Council to take up the two sheriffs and their accomplices, to be prosecuted at law, using force if necessary; they were accordingly sent to the Tower, but afterwards (on Habeas Corpus) bailed, prosecuted, convicted, and fined.[1]

At an adjourned meeting the opposition party, supposing they had obtained their end, failed to appear in sufficient numbers, and Sir Ralph Box's election was carried, but Box was frightened and paid off; finally, North and Rice entered upon office.

For this, together with the alleged liberty of unlicensed printing on the part of the City, the charter of the City of London was declared forfeited.

Of this, says Stowe,

Many did make but a matter of sport, and songs were merrily sung at entertainments in the City on this occasion to the tune of Packington Pound:

> Ye freemen, and masters, and prentices mourn
> For now you are left with your charter forlorn,
> Since London was London, I dare boldly say,
> For your riots you never so dearly did pay.
>   In Westminster Hall
>   Your Dagon did fall
> That caused you to rise and mutiny all.

---

[1] Principals 2,000*l*., bail 1,000*l*.; Pilkington, because in prison, 500*l*.; other 1,000 and 500 marks.

THE COMPANY OF SKINNERS. 71

The cause was twice tried before the Lord Chancellor on a writ of
quo warranto, first by Mr. Finch, the King's Solicitor for the Crown,
and Sir George Troby, the Recorder for the City; and, again, by Sir
Robert Simpes, the King's Attorney-general, and Mr. Pollexfen for the
City.

Evelyn tells us[1] that he was present on the occasion when the Lord
Mayor, Sheriff, and Aldermen, presented a humble petition to his
Majesty on the quo warranto against the charter, which they delivered
to his Majesty in the Presence Chamber, after which the King returned
into the Council Chamber, when the Mayor and his brethren were
called in—

And my Lord Keeper made a speech to them exaggerating the disorderly and
riotous behaviour in the late election and polling for Papilion and Du Bois after
the Common Hall had been finally dissolved, with other misdemeanours and libels
on the Government, &c., and that but for the submission, and under such as the
King should require their obedience to, he would certainly enter judgment against
them, which hitherto he had suspended.

The things required were as follows: that they should neither elect Maior,
Sheriff, Aldermen, Recorder, Common Serjeant, Town Cleark, Coroner, or
Steward of Southwark without his Majesty's approbation, and that if they presented any his Majesty did not like they should proceed in wonted manner to a
second choiss; if that was disapproved his Majesty to nominate them, and if
within five days they thought good to assent to them all former miscarriages
should be forgotten.[2]

In the last years of James II., when he was in apprehension of the
Prince of Orange invading England, he appointed Lord Jefferies, at
that time Lord Chancellor (who himself had been instrumental in pro-
curing judgment against the City) to carry back the charter to
Guildhall in great formality, hoping thereby, adds Stowe,[3] "to sweeten
the City," who were weary of his government. After the accession of
William and Mary the City presented a petition to their Majesties
praying for the passing an Act for the restoration of the City charter.
This made Pilkington the most popular man of the day.

On the occasion of his accepting the civic chair in 1689[4] both King
William and Queen Mary honoured him with their presence, together
with the Prince and Princess of Denmark, all the principal officers of
the Court and both Houses of Parliament, the Bishop of London and

[1] Evelyn's Diary, June 18, 1683.   [2] Vol. i. 553.
[3] Stowe, p. 78.
[4] Herbert, p. 326.

prelates of the Church, the Lords Commissioners of the Privy Seal, the Lord Chief Justices of both Benches, the Lord Baron, and all the other Judges, the four Dutch and all foreign Ambassadors, Envoyes, and Attaches.

A copy of the pageant which was enacted on that occasion is in the Guildhall Library, all set forth at the proper costs and charges of the Right Worshipful Company of Skinners, by Mathew Trautman.[1]

The following lines are selected as a specimen of the time; Mercy in a robe of crimson and silver mantle addresses his Lordship in these words:

> Since first Augusta was mine ancient name,
> London has more than once been in a flame,
> Our fierce elections, our domestic wars,
> Our hot contentions, and our civil jars,
> In a few years have prejudiced us more
> Then all the Jesuits' powder did before;
> But, thanks my Lord, the cloud is now dispersed,
> And we are of our former rights possessed.
> The Sun, with you, resumes its course this year,
> And shines again within our hemisphere;
> All we enjoy we must acknowledge due
> To England's Great PRESERVER, and to you:
> You did assert our privileges. He
> Timely redeemed from pointed Tyranny!
> You for our freedom sacrificed your own.
> What more could Pompey for his Rome have done?
> In some degree to make you recompense
> Behold, Peace, Concord, Mercy, Innocence:
> These are the best supporters of a state,
> My handmaids here, on you assigned to wait.

The following is one of the songs used on another occasion, in 1691:—

> Come boys drink an health to the chiefs of the City,
> The loyal Lord Mayor and the Legal Committee.
> The Imperial City, this year that with you
> Hath restored us our lives and our liberties too.
>
> With justice and peace may it ever be floating,
> May the heads that support it agree in their voting,
> May a strong tide of union still flow in your hall,
> And no sea of faction ere beat down your wall.

---

[1] Tanburn, p. 306.

A health to the dons of the Company's table,
Crown every bumper with ermine and sable,
If ermine's the emblem of honour, then you,
As well as their lordships, are dignified too.

From heats and contentions for ever be free,
Let City and Court make one harmony.
May never more discord among you be found,
But one loyal bumper for ever go round.

Sir HUMPHREY EDWIN, or EDWYN, son of William Edwin, Sheriff 1688, elected Mayor and Alderman of Tower Ward 22 October, 1689, Barber Surgeon, afterwards Skinner.

Arms: Argent, a cross flory engrailed, between four Cornish choughs sable.

He was descended from the Edwyns of Hereford and Glamorgan; Lord Mayor temp. William III. A.D. 1697-8. His son and heir, by his wife Elizabeth Sambrooke, Samuel Edwin, of Llanfihangel, in the county of Glamorgan, married Lady Catherine Montagne, third daughter of the Earl of Manchester. Died 14 December, 1707. Edith, daughter of Sir Humphrey, married William Coney of Walpole, Norfolk, who died in 1742 at the ripe age of 82; their son Edwin became High Sheriff of Norfolk in 1734, died in 1755, aged 68; his son Robert, Colonel of the Norfolk Militia, married Anne Bright; their daughter Elizabeth married Walter Swaine, esq., of Levering-ton; Louisa, daughter and coheiress of the latter, became united to Charles Whiting, esq., of Romford, whose fourth daughter married E. J. Sage, esq., at present a resident in Stoke Newington, and to whom I am indebted for the foregoing particulars.

As soon as the country had settled back upon its old foundations the persecution of the Dissenters was resumed with more rigour than ever, and it was enacted [1] that no person should be elected to any office in the corporation of a town unless he should have within one year before his election received the sacrament in the form prescribed by the Church. Those who invented this precaution flattered themselves that no real Dissenter would be able to pass such an ordeal. It was followed up in 1673 by the Test Act, which imposed the same

[1] Wyon's *History of Queen Anne*, p. 133.

obligation. The Act of Toleration with which William commenced his reign did nothing more than clear away some harsh statutes which rendered Dissenters liable to a heavy fine for visiting a conventicle, but it did not remove the obstacles which stood in their way to office. In 1697 the choice of the City fell upon Sir Humphrey Edwin to be Lord Mayor. He took the sacrament in the form prescribed by the Corporation Act. He was in consequence installed in his office, and he then openly proclaimed himself a Dissenter by resorting to a conventicle in full civic state, with the sword and mace borne before him.

At a Court of Aldermen, held on the 9th of November,[1] attention was drawn to the fact that Sir Humphrey Edwin, the then Lord Mayor, had on the two previous afternoons of the Lord's day gone to a private meeting-house, and a resolution was passed at the court, that a restraint be put to the proceeding, and that the like practice be not permitted for the time to come.

Attention having been drawn to the subject by this flagrant case it soon became a matter of notoriety that Edwin was by no means the only Dissenter who had obtained office by submitting to a single act of conformity with the Established Church. The various corporations of the City swarmed with occasional conformists. There were Dissenters holding lucrative places in the magistracy, the customs, the excise, the army and navy, and even the royal household. This led to the passing of the Act for preventing occasional conformity.

Sir Humphrey Edwin appears to have not only gained the approval of his fellow citizens, but well and fully to have realised and met the difficulties of the times in which he lived, and the duties to which he had been called.

He acted zealously and energetically in carrying out an order of their Lords Excellencies in Council which had been forwarded to the Lord Mayor and Court of Aldermen,[2] wherein they were instructed to search for and seize certain desperate and dangerous persons who had come into the kingdom from foreign parts, and who had been concerned in the late horrid conspiracy of Sir George Barclay, Sir John Fenwick, and others, to assassinate his Majesty's sacred person, for which purpose thirty-six warrants were issued.

The search was ordered to commence November 11, at four o'clock.

[1] Rep. 102.
[2] Court of Aldermen, Rep. 102, Nov. 11, 1694.

THE COMPANY OF SKINNERS. 75

"Great (says Macaulay[1]) was the dismay amongst the Jacobites; those who had betted deep on the constancy of Louis took to flight; one unfortunate zealot of divine right drowned himself . . . . but the rage and mortification were confined to a very small minority. Never since the Restoration had there been such times of public gladness in every part of the kingdom; peace was proclaimed, and the general sentiment was manifested by banquets, pageants, loyal healths, beating of drums, and blowing of trumpets, and breaking up of hogsheads."

The 4th of November, which was the anniversary of the King's birthday, and the 5th that of his landing at Torbay, were celebrated with bonfires and crackers all over the country. After some days of anxious expectation his Majesty landed at Margate on the 14th of November. A meeting of the Court of Aldermen[2] was summoned for the following day, at which it was arranged that the Lord Mayor, wearing his rich collar and jewels uncovered, the Aldermen and Sheriffs, should ride and meet his Majesty at the Sessions House, Saint Margaret's Hill, Southwark, on the morning of the 16th. The route was through "Queen Street, Budge Roe, and Cannon Street." On arriving at the Sessions House Sir Humphrey Edwin presented to his Majesty the City sword, which his Majesty graciously returned to Sir Humphrey, who bore it before him in the procession. His Majesty's coach was attended in his journey through the City by all the City officers in new liveries, the Duke of Gloucester, and Prince George. The right and left-hand side of Cheapside was lined with the Livery Companies with their standards; the Skinners[3] to the number of 200 being stationed at the east end of Golden Lane; at the east of Saint Paul's churchyard stood the boys of Christ's Hospital; round the Cathedral, down Ludgate Hill and Fleet Street, were drawn up three regiments of Londoners; from Temple Bar to Whitehall Gate the trainbands of Middlesex and the foot-guards were under arms; tapestry, ribands, and flags decorated the route, and the windows were filled with a delighted and enthusiastic multitude. With such indications of joy and affection was he greeted from the beginning to the end of his journey, that William wrote that evening to his friend Heinsius, "I never saw such a multitude of well-dressed people."

At a Council held a few hours after his public entry, the 2nd of

[1] Vol. iv. p. 803.
[2] Ibid.   [3] Ibid. p. 806.

December was appointed as a day of thanksgiving for the peace,[1] and the Chapter of Saint Paul's resolved that the choir of the Cathedral, which had slowly risen to supply the place of the former one, should be opened. William announced his intention of being present, but when it was represented to him that three hundred thousand people would assemble to see him pass he abandoned his intention and went to his private chapel in Whitehall, where Bishop Burnet preached. In the City the Lord Mayor, Sir Humphrey Edwin, and all the City magistrates, attended service in the Cathedral, and an eloquent sermon was delivered by Bishop Compton,[2] who took his text from Psalm cxxii. " I was glad when they said unto me, Let us go into the house of the Lord."

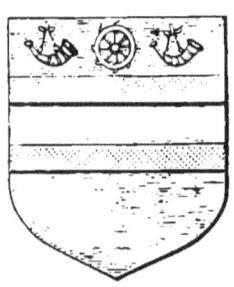

Sir GEORGE MERTTINS, knt. 1724, son of — Merttins of Cornhill, goldsmith and jeweller, and descendant of a family of that name in Frankfort, Germany.

Arms: Azure, two bars or, in chief a Catherine wheel, between as many bugle-horns argent.

Sir George was Alderman of Bridge Ward, knighted 11 April, 1713, Lord Mayor 1724, treasurer of Christ's Hospital and afterwards president; died in 1727, shortly after his elevation to the latter office; was buried in the south cloister of Christ's Church, Newgate Street, 11 November, 1727, with his wife Philadelphia, whose death had preceded him by about five years, and by whom he had issue. She was the daughter of John Mitford, of Stratford-le-Bow, Middlesex, third son of Robert Mitford, esq., of Mitford Castle, Northumberland.

Sir George's only brother, Henry Merttins, was of Valence, in the parish of Dagenham, Essex, and of the city of London, jeweller. He was buried at Dagenham in 1725, aged 66.[3]

[1] Signed at Ryswick, 10 Sept. 1697.

[2] Henry Compton, Bishop of London, was the second son of Spencer Compton, second Earl of Northampton. He witnessed the laying of the first stone of the Cathedral, as well as its completion. He died in February, 1713, in the eighty-first year of his age.—Elmes's *History of Sir Christopher Wren.*

[3] Extracted from his MS. collections by the kind permission of E. J. Sage, esq., compiled from the registers of Dagenham, Barking Manor Court Rolls, Harrison MSS., &c., &c.

THE COMPANY OF SKINNERS. 77

Sir CHARLES ASGILL, Bart., Mayor 1757. Alderman of Candlewick Ward.

Arms: Per fesse argent and vert, a pale countercharged, in each piece of the first a lion's head erased gules.[1]

Sir ROBERT KITE, knt., Mayor 1766. Master 1756. Grandfather of Alexander Ball.

Arms: Azure, a chevron between three kites' heads erased or. See p. 36.

It would not be right if in concluding our account of the illustrious members of the Company who have filled the office of Mayor we omitted some account of others who by their benefactions and charities have given encouragement to the industrious, aid to the student, or assistance to the poor.

In 1557 Mr. Thomas Hunt left lands which then produced 60*l*. per annum, to lend freely to such young men and occupiers, free of the Company, as had served at least eight years' apprenticeship, and two years as journeymen for wages, one sum of 20*l*. for three years at an interest of 2½*l*. per cent., and when the profit of the land to be bought by the residue of the estate should amount to 400*l*. it should be lent to twenty young men, and the residue to relieve five poor decayed freemen of the Company. By the prudent management of the Company the funds have been considerably increased, and afford aid and assistance to twenty-six poor freemen, or their widows, besides contributing capital to aid young men commencing business.

In 1588 Mr. Lawrence Atwell left land and tenements to form a stock from time to time to be employed in some good sort whereby

---

[1] It does not appear that these were the arms borne by Sir Charles Asgill. They were granted to the family in the year 1821. He resided at Richmond, Surrey, in a good house by the river-side. This villa is mentioned in Lysons as having become the property of Whitshed Keene, esq. and that it is described in the lease as being on the site of the ancient palace. There is a print of it in the *Vitruvius Britannicus*, vol. iv. p. 74.

poor people, especially such as were free of the Company, might be set on work. The funds of this estate have largely increased, and loans free of interest are lent for a period of two years to persons commencing business.

In 1618 Sir James Lancaster left certain lands in the county of Lincoln to the Company in trust for the town of Basingstoke, and towards the maintenance of four poor scholars. By an order of the Court of Chancery, 1713, this trust was relegated to the Corporation of Basingstoke, who remit to the Company the amount bequeathed for the payment of poor scholars, of which two, value 16*l.* per annum each, are appointed to Oxford, and two to Cambridge.

In 1619 Sir Thomas Smith, besides the portion of his property which relates to Tonbridge School, bequeathed to the Company certain property, to pay yearly to the five parishes of Bidborough, Tonbridge, Speldhurst, Otley, and Sutton-at-Hone, Kent, 5*l.* 10*s.* each, to be paid to the churchwardens for the poorest and honestest resident householders thereof; also a sum of 20*s.* worth of cloth to form a winter garment; and as the revenue increased the charity was to be extended to Darenth, Wilmington, Otford, and Shorne. Application has been made to the Charity Commissioners for a new scheme for this portion of the trust. Under this will six Exhibitions are given away to poor scholars at the University, each of the annual value of 17*l.* per annum.

In 1630 John Meredith bequeathed certain properties to pay yearly to aged freemen and freemen's widows; also 5*l.* to two unbeneficed clergymen of the Church of England; of these latter recipients four are now appointed who receive 20*l.* a year each.

In 1611 William Stoddart left 2,000 marks for the relief of the poor of the Company, and maintaining and educating the sons of poor freemen at Christ's Hospital. The bequest was paid to the treasurer of Christ's Hospital for the time being, and the Company nominate ten children for education.

ALMSHOUSES.

In addition to the school at Tonbridge, Sir Andrew Judd made a provision under his will for founding and endowing an almshouse in St. Helen's Close, in the City of London, for six poor freemen of the Company. The almshouses were rebuilt by the Company in 1729, J. Phillips being Master.

Dame Alice Smith also left a bequest to these almshouses, A.D. 1592. Each freeman, besides lodging, receives a pension of 20l. per annum, with coals.

In 1663, Mr. Lewis Newbury, after leaving 100l. to be lent to poor freemen and 50l. to the Company, directed that so much of his estate as should be got in should be laid out in the purchase of a piece of ground and building of so many small houses for six poor women, to be appointed by the Company. The almshouses, sufficient for the accommodation of twelve poor widows, with chapel, and rooms for the minister, were afterwards erected at Mile End, A.D. 1688, Benjamin Alexander, Master. Each pensioner receives 20l. per annum with coals.

Bishop Beccles now acts as Chaplain to the Company and the almshouses.

The Company[1] have recently given two Exhibitions of 60l. per annum to liverymen and freemen of the Company.

One of 50l. to the Middle Class School Corporation.
One of 30l. to the London School Board.
One of 50l. to the City of London School.
One of 40l. to the National School of Music.

MANOR OF PELLIPAR, AND CONNECTION OF THE SKINNERS WITH IRELAND.

Nor should we omit to mention the connection of the Skinners' Company with the Society of Governors and Assistants of London for the planting of Ulster, better known perhaps as the Irish Society, to whom James the First, after the suppression of the Irish rebellion, A.D. 1609, gave his licence to hold lands in mortmain. This grant we afterwards find Charles the First endeavoured to repeal, A.D. 1630, whereupon a petition was presented by the Lord Mayor and the Companies of the City of London not only to his Majesty but also to the House of Commons. After some proceedings had been taken in the Star Chamber, an arrangement was effected between the Society and his Majesty, and the twelve chief Companies met and contributed

---

[1] February 8th 1798, the Company voted 1,000l. per annum towards the expense of carrying on the war.

40,000*l.*, in equal proportions of 3,333*l.* 6*s.* 8*d.* each. In their contribution the Skinners were assisted by three other Companies, viz., the Stationers, Bakers, and Girdlers. The total amount ultimately expended in Ireland was, however, much larger, for we find it stated in the petition which was presented to the Commons by the Society, that not less a sum than 130,000*l.* had been expended, irrespective of many thousands laid out by the tenants.

It appears that the persons selected by the City and the twelve chief City Companies to view the intended plantation consisted of Mr. John Board, goldsmith, Hugh Hammersley, haberdasher, Robert Tresswell, painter stainer,[1] and John Rowley, draper. Three hundred pounds were allotted for their expenses of viewing the land, to which another one hundred pounds was afterwards added. Their report was referred to a committee of the City and twelve Companies to consider. It was agreed that there should be expended by the City on the plantation a sum of 20,000*l.* according to the assessment set upon every Company to the corn-rate; whereof 15,000*l.* was to be expended on the plantation. And provided for the building of three hundred houses in Derry and two hundred in Coleraine, and for the walls and fortifications thereof, with four thousand acres next adjacent, exclusive of waste and bog added thereto. That the keeping of Cutmore Castle should belong to the City, together with wood, timber, trees, and fisheries in the Ban and Lough Foyle. That for the ordering and conducting of the plantation a Company should be established by charter (1613), which should consist of one governor and twenty-four assistants, and further that the governor and five of the assistants should be aldermen of the City of London. The first governor elected under the charter was Alderman Sir William Cokayne, Citizen and Skinner.

The new city (says Macaulay)[2] soon arose, which on account of its connection with the City of London was called London-derry; the buildings covered the slope of the hill which overlooked the Foyle. On the highest ground stood the cathedral, and near it the bishop's palace.

The dwellings were encompassed by a wall, of which the whole circumference was little less than a mile; on the bastions were placed culverins and sakers presented by the wealthy guilds of London and

[1] Not a member of one of the twelve City Companies.
[2] Vol. iii. p. 12.

the colony. On some of these guns, which have done memorable service to the great cause, the devices of the Fishmongers', Vintners', and Merchant Taylors' Company are still discernible; that which is said to have been presented by the Skinners is supposed to have been shipped as ballast to America; at all events the cannon cannot be identified Of the celebrated siege which it afterwards sustained the reader cannot do better than refer to Macaulay.

There is something quaint and singular in the way in which these lands were made over to the twelve companies. After a careful survey they were divided into what was considered twelve equal proportions, as in the case of the twelve tribes, and lots were drawn by all the Companies, which decided the right of proprietorship.

The portion allotted to the Skinners is known as the Manor of Pellipar, the nearest point of which is about four miles west of Londonderry. It consists of the parishes of Upper and Lower Cumber, Banacher, Dungiven, Ballynascreen, containing about 44,450 acres; of this about 20,756 are at present under cultivation, and the rest consists of mountain, moor, and bog. Benbradagh, which stands close to Dungiven, rises to a height of 1,517 feet, and the White Mountain to 1,773 feet, above the sea.

The market town of Dungiven is about fourteen miles from Derry, and is situated on the River Roe. The original castle was pulled down 1803, and rebuilt by Robert Ogilby, esq. who died before its completion. The town consists of one long and one cross street of about 112 houses, together with church and market-house, Presbyterian meeting-house, and Roman Catholic chapel, &c. Pellipar House, a handsome residence, is at present occupied by Mr. James Ogilby, Strangemore by Mr. King, and others by the Company's agent, Mr. James Clarke, Canon Ross, &c.

Close to the town of Dungiven is an interesting Dolmen or Pillar Stone. The object of erecting these stones, called also Maenhir, or Gallaun, has been the subject of much discussion; there are many such in the North of Ireland, although none that I am aware of approaching in size or importance those of Brittany.

The mound is raised about five feet above the level of the hill, truncated at the top, and about fifteen feet in diameter; the stone is five feet high by an average width of two feet nine inches, and in thickness about one foot, with pointed and round end, much like a large celt-stone standing with its edge upward.

f

A DOLMEN OR PILLAR-STONE, ERECTED CLOSE TO THE TOWN OF DUNGIVEN.

I was struck with the pointed shadow which it cast on the circular earthen ring surrounding the mound, and, on consulting a compass, found it stood with the thin sides due north and south; the thought struck me, that if at any time it was used as a gnomon there would be a pointer for the shadow to fall on at noon; and on further examining the mound I discovered on the south side, not many points removed from its position, a smaller stone which, I have no doubt, served as a pointer, as there were no other stones visible or around the mound.

I mentioned this circumstance to Mr. Hunt, the County Surveyor of Tyrone, who informed me, now his attention had been drawn to it, that he recollected that many of these stones stood north and south. If so, here is clearly another use for these singular stones other than those of burial.

To the south of the stone, within three hundred feet or more, lies the Roman Catholic Chapel of St. Columba, on the banks of the River Roe.

It is possible that St. Columba may have preached Christianity here, and that the rite of baptism was administered on the river,

To face page 83.

where a church was afterwards erected: of this church the ruined chancel still remains, together with a chancel arch and nave.[1]

The annexed illustration represents the tomb or monument in the chancel of Covey Na Gall. There is an arch nine feet high, and beneath a recumbent figure, and sculptures in niches, said to represent his sons. Covey na Gall, or, as he is called in Erse, Cuncigh na Gall, or the Stranger, was of the tribe of O'Chans, whose territories had been confiscated; he died 1385.

The county is said to have been originally called Glen Given, or Glen of Skins, and from its stronghold it took the name of Dun Given, from *Dun* a fort, and *Given* a skin.

SCHEDULE OF ORNAMENTAL PLATE EXHIBITED AT SKINNERS' HALL, 1874.

The following account of the plate in the possession of the Skinners' Company is taken from the Catalogue of Antiquities and Works of Art exhibited at Ironmongers' Hall in 1861.[2] I am permitted by the editor, Mr. George Russell French, to reproduce the description, and to his kindness I am likewise indebted for the loan of the accompanying illustrations.

A ROSEWATER DISH, silver gilt, diameter 19½ inches, weight 76 oz. In the raised centre is the coat of arms of the Company with their supporters, crest, and motto, surrounded by the inscription, which is repeated on the rim, "The Guift of Mr. Francis Cowell (Covell) Skynner, deceased the 7th of Septr. 1625." Plate-mark the small black letter *i* for 1566, with the initials R. V. on a shield with a heart below.

THE BRETON LOVING CUP,[3] silver gilt, standing on a baluster stem,

---

[1] The ruins present features in most respects similar to the church of Killea in Kintyre, Scotland, drawn and described by Captain T. P. White, R.E., F.R.S.

[2] Vol. ii. pp. 585, 590.

[3] The loving cup was in Saxon called huæp, and the ceremony is one of great antiquity. It consisted in two or more persons drinking from the same goblet. He who first drinks before doing so cries out Waes hel, and he who receives the cup before drinking responds Driuk hel. (Dictée du Mobilier, vol. ii. p. 115).

12½ inches high, weight 29 oz. The bowl is ornamented with the arms and crest of the Company, and round the rim is inscribed, "Ex dono et in testimonium grati animi Georgij Breton olim Clerici inclitæ Societatis Pellipariorum, London;" and on a corresponding oval, "qui obijt vicesimo nono die Februaij, 1639." Plate-mark the court-hand N, standing for 1650, with the lion passant and leopard's head, and the initials W. M. on a shield with a Moor's head.

THE POWELL CUP, similar in shape to Breton's cup. It is a "loving cup" of silver gilt, and weighs 26 oz. It is inscribed, "The gift of Mr. Edward Powell, Citizen and Skinner of London, 1654," with the arms of the Company on one side, and on the other a coat, Quarterly, 1 and 4, party per fess or and argent, a lion rampant; Gules, 2 and 3, six pheons 3, 2, and 1. Crest: On a helmet an estoile. The plate-mark, the Lombardic letter V, answers to the date 1616, with the lion passant and leopard's head, and the initial F.

A SILVER GILT LOVING CUP, similar to Breton's cup, inscribed, "Ex dono Gulielmi Ridges, Armigeri, 13 Octo, 1670." On one side is a shield of arms having "three demi-lions ermine." On the other side is a crest, a demi-lion ermine, holding in his dexter paw a battle-axe. The plate-mark is the Lombardic letter V, for the year 1616, with the initials R. F. on a heart-shaped shield.

Viollet le Duc gives the following illustration, taken from an old work of the twelfth century, entitled li Romans de Brut:

"Costume est, sire en son païs (des Saxons)
Quant ami boivent entre ami.
Que cil dist *wes hel* qui doit boire
Et cil drinkel qui doit recoivre;
Dont boit cil tote la moitie
Et por joie et por amistié;
Au hanap rescoivre et baillier
Est costume d'entre baisier.
Li rois si com il li aprist,
Dist trinkel et si sosrist;
Provent but et puis li bailla.
Et en baillant le roi baisa."

also in Roman de Parise la duchesse, a unique MS. in the Bibliothèque impériale:

"Li roi demande l'aive ou palais princiner
Quant il orent lavé s'asistrent au dîner
A la plu maitre table sert Hugues de vin clere,
A l'enap qui fu d'or conques ne fu blamez."

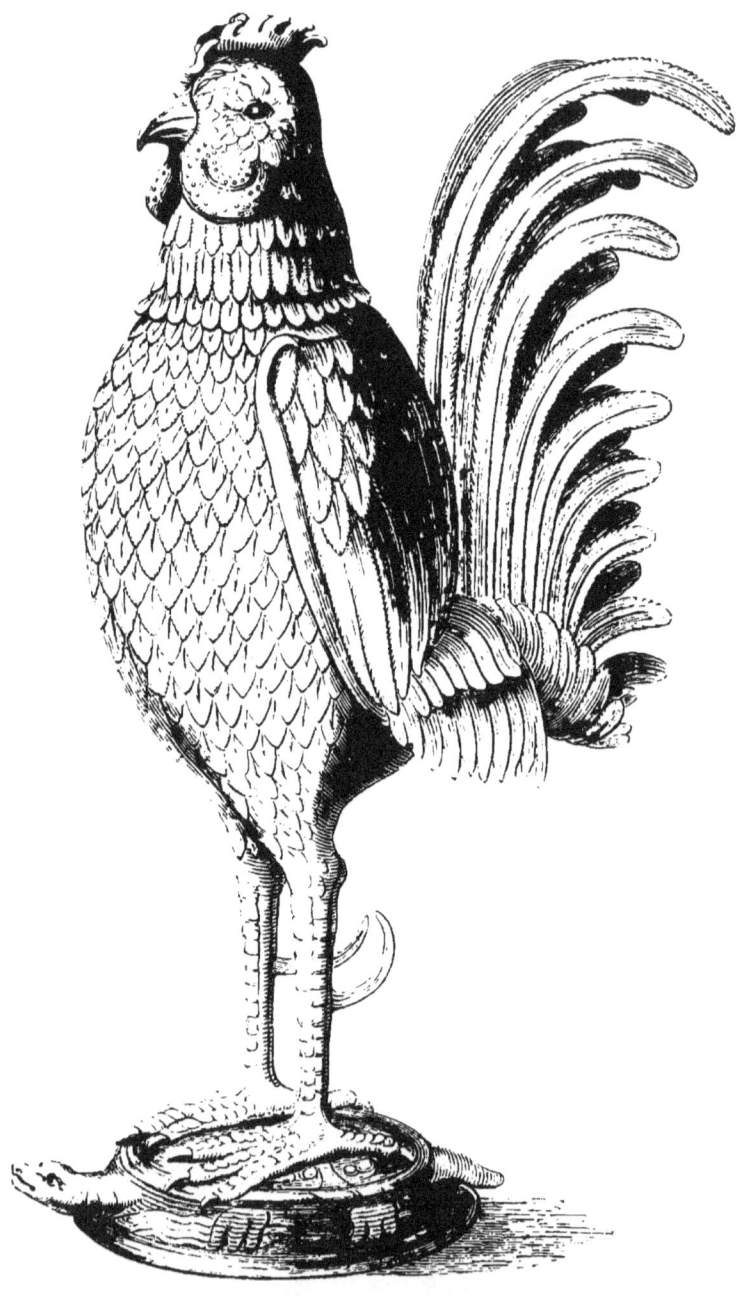

LOVING CUP. THE GIFT OF SIR RICHARD COKAYNE, KNT., CIRCA 1619.

THE GIFT OF MARY DAUGHTER OF RICHARD ROBINSON,
and wife to Thomas Smith and John Peacock, Skinners.

The FIVE COKAYNE LOVING CUPS, silver gilt, in the form of cocks, of which the heads must be removed for the purpose of drinking. The cocks are placed on the backs of turtles; each cup is 16½ inches high, and weighs 72 oz. These birds were bequeathed to the Company by the will of Mr. William Cockayne, dated 24th October, 41 Elizabeth (1598). On the receipt of the cocks the Company covenanted with Mr. Cockayne's executors that "they and their successors would thereafter use the said five Guift Cups to be borne upon their Election-day of Master and Wardens every year before the Wardens of the said Mystery for the Election of Master and Wardens, according to the true meaning of the will of the said Wm. Cockayne deceased;" which has been the invariable custom ever since. These cups are designed in the spirit of the time of the sixteenth century, having the punning allusion to the donor's name, as also in the instance of the "Peacock Cup" described below. Much of the plate of this period was made in the shape of animals and birds. In the fine collection of Lord Londesborough, among other designs, are to be seen cocks and peacocks. The plate-mark is the small black letter ḣ, for the year 1565, with a lion passant guardant and leopard's head, with the letter G on a shield.

The PEACOCK CUP. A silver peahen with two peachicks; one other is lost. It forms a "loving cup" on the head being removed; it is 16¼ inches high, and weighs 62 oz. 10 dwts. On the foot of the cup is a coat of arms, In a lozenge, a chevron ermine between three esquires' helmets. The ground of the foot is embossed with figures of reptiles, turtles, snails, and tree-roots. On the base is inscribed, "The gifte of Mary, ye davghter of Richard Robinson, and wife to Thomas Smith and James Peacock, Skinn^{ers}, 1642." There is no plate-mark.

The BATEMAN CUP, silver gilt, on baluster stem 12¼ inches high, weight 27 oz., inscribed "The gifte of ye Wrp'll Robert Bateman, Brother of this Company, and late Chamberlaine of ye Hon'ble Citty of London. Who deceased ye 11th Decem. 1644." On one side of the cup are the arms and crest of the Company, and on the opposite side is the coat of arms of the donor, viz. "Or, three starres, issuant from as many cressants gules," which coat, Gwillim says, was borne by "Robert Bateman, Esquier, Chamberlain of London, who left a hopefull and flourishing issue, viz. Richard Bateman, William Bateman, Anthony Bateman, now Sheriff of London 1658, and Thomas

Bateman, all Merchants and Members of that noble City." Of these sons Anthony was Lord Mayor in 1664, and was knighted; and Thomas was created a baronet in 1644, but died without issue. The plate-mark is the court-hand letter B, for the year 1639, with the lion passant and leopard's head, and on a heart-shaped shield is a mullet between five bezants, and on the upper part the initials D. W. On the cup is the Bateman crest, viz. a star issuant from a crescent.

A SILVER SALT, of octagonal form, height 9 inches, width at base 10¼ inches, weight 66 oz. 10 dwts. The foot is ornamented with the arms of the Company and a shield bearing, " On a cross five eagles displayed." On the top is inscribed, " The Gifte of Ben. Albin, Esq. late Cittizen and Skinner, of London, dec^d Anno dom. 1676." The plate-mark is obliterated. There is a shield with the initials W. P. and an estoile. On the rim of the salt are four projections or horns, which seem to have been for the purpose of supporting a covering, most probably a napkin, as it was considered desirable to keep the cover clear of the salt itself; " loke that your salte seller lydde touch not the salte," saith " the Boke of Kervinge."

A PAIR OF SILVER GILT LOVING CUPS, each of which is 12 inches high, 6 inches diameter: each weighs 37 oz. and is ornamented with repoussé work, on baluster stem, having on a shield of arms " three bowls, issuant from each a boar's head erect." On the rim is inscribed, " The gifte of Edward Bolle, Esqr, one of the Company of Skinners, 168$^0_1$." The plate-mark, the small black letter f, stands for 1680, with the lion passant and leopard's head, and the letters J. B. on a shield bezantée. This worthy citizen was, no doubt, of the ancient family of Bolle, extinct baronets, of Scampton, whose principal seat was at Bolle Hall, in Swineshead, co. Lincoln. Sir George Bolle, knt., was Lord Mayor of London in 1617, and by his wife Jane, daughter and coheir of Sir John Hart, knt., Lord Mayor in 1590, had a son John, who was created a baronet in 1628. The title became extinct in the fourth generation in 1714.

They had for arms, " Azure, three bowls or, out of each a boar's head erect argent." It appears that an ancestor of the family was Alan de Swineshead, lord of the manor of Bolle Hall, hence the canting nature of the arms. It was at the abbey of Cistercian monks at Swineshead that King John was taken ill.

SNUFF-BOX. THE GIFT OF ROGER P. KEMP, 1680.

"*Messenger.* My lord, your valiant kinsman, Falconbridge,
  Desires your Majesty to leave the field
  And send him word by me which way you go.
K. John. Tell him, towards Swinestead, to the Abbey there."
  Shakespeare's *King John*, Act v., Scene 3.

Shakespeare gives the popular version of his death taking place there:

"The King, I fear, is poisoned by a monk."—Scene 6.

The true name of the place where King John was taken ill was not Swinestead, which is in a different part of Lincolnshire, but Swineshead, which is in the direct route from Lynn Regis to Sleaford, where the King rested, and to Newark, where he died. Not a restige remains of the abbey, which was founded in 1134 by Robert de Gresley; a mansion was built from its ruins by one of the Lackton family, according to Dugdale.

A SILVER LEOPARD, collared, representing the crest of the Company and forming a snuff-box, of which the head is contrived to contain one kind of snuff and the body to hold another. Around the collar is inscribed, "The guift of Roger Kemp, Master, 1680." Weight 34 oz.

A large SILVER FLAGON and COVER $12\frac{1}{2}$ inches high, 6 inches diameter, weight 32 oz. The purchase of the Cover has a winged demi-female, terminating in foliage. It is inscribed, "The guift of William Russell, Esq., free of the Worshipfull Company of Skinners, Ap^r 16, 1679." The date-mark is the small text g for 1684. It has the arms and motto of the Company.

A SILVER SALVER, $14\frac{1}{4}$ inches in diameter, weight 45 oz. standing on a foot $3\frac{1}{2}$ inches high, ornamented with the arms, supporters, and motto of the Company, inscribed, "The gift of Mr. Lewis Newberry, Skinner, An° Dom' 1684." Date-mark, small text g for 1684.

A SILVER TANKARD, $7\frac{1}{2}$ inches high, $5\frac{1}{2}$ inches diameter, weight 49 oz., inscribed, "The gift of Sir Richard Chiverton, Kn^t and Alderman, a Member of this Company, 1686," with the arms, crest, supporters, and motto of the Company. The date-mark is the small text letter h for the year 1685.

A Silver Bowl or Monteith, diameter 13 inches, depth 6¼ inches, weight 72 oz. 6 dwts., inscribed, "The gift of Sir Richard Chiverton, Kn⁴ and Alderman, a Member of this Company, 1686," with the arms and motto of the Company. The donor was Lord Mayor of London in 1658, and bore for arms, Argent, a tower tripple-towered sable, on a mount proper.

Sir Richard Chiverton, who was knighted by Oliver Cromwell, was the second son of Richard Chiverton of Trehensye, co. Cornwall, and his wife Isabel, daughter of ———— Polewhele of Polewhele, in the same county.

At the entrance of a small cross aisle on the south side of Quethiock Church, Cornwall, belonging to the manor of Trehunsey, are placed against the wall the brasses of Chiverton, his wife, and eleven children; also the arms of Chiverton impaling Polewhele. Richard Chiverton died 28 July, 1617, and Isabel his wife died 25 May, 1631. The date-mark is the same as on the tankard, viz., the small text b for 1685, with the lion passant and leopard's head, and the initials G. G. on a shield.

A Silver Snuffer Stand with Snuffers, inscribed, "The gift of S' Will Russell, K*, deceased." The snuffers have the arms of the Company, and on the box is inscribed as above; they fit into the stand somewhat in the form of a candle. The plate-mark is the court-hand W, with Britannia and lion's head erased. 1705.

Two Silver Candlesticks in form of an Italian Doric column with extended base, 12½ inches high, exclusive of arms, ornamented with the arms of the Company, and weighing 25 oz. It has been mounted with scroll branches forming a candelabrum for three lights. The gift of Sir William Russel, knt. 1705.

Two other Silver Candlesticks, 15 inches in height, somewhat similar to the other two, mounted with scroll branches, to form a centre, 35 oz. 1752.

Four small Baluster Candlesticks of silver, with inscription "Ex dono Societat. Angl. ad Indos Orientalis Negotiant." They were presented about the year 1690.

A Silver Gilt Tankard, diameter 5 inches, height 6¾, weight 31 oz. 10 dwts., elaborately ornamented in repoussé work, having the arms of the Company engraved in front, the supporter on the dexter side being a leopard, and on the sinister a leopard or wolf collared.

SNUFFER STAND.

THE GIFT OF WM. RUSSEL, KNT.

It is inscribed, "The gift of James Langdon Reynolds, Citizen and Skinner, Corpus Christi, 1646." The plate-mark, a small black letter ı, would give the year 1646 for the date of the tankard; it has the lion passant and leopard's head, and on an oval shield between a crown and a leopard's head are the initials I. R.

A handsome SILVER-GILT ROSEWATER DISH, $17\frac{1}{2}$ inches in diameter, elaborately wrought in repoussée with a scroll and flowers, with inner-raised surface similarly wrought. The arms of the Company and donor are engraved on the border; the centre carries the following inscription:

> This piece of Plate
> is presented to the
> Worshipful Company of Skinners,
> by Thomas Moore, Esqre.
> To commemorate the Coronation of
> His Majesty George the Fourth,
> on Thursday the 19th day of July, 1821,
> at which ceremony he had the honor of representing
> that Company
> as one of the twelve
> Citizens of London,
> to the
> Chief Butler of England.[1]

Weight 40 oz.; letter ƀ, 1685.

A SILVER CENTRE-PIECE elaborately wrought, with extended branches for either fruit or flowers, stands 24 inches in height, on a raised plateau 15 inches in diameter, with supporters holding shields engraved with the arms of the Company and donor; weight 158 oz., date 1829; on the base is engraved the following inscription:

> 1862.
> Presented to the
> Worshipful Company of Skinners
> by Thomas Kensit, Esq.
> Clerk of the Company,
> in testimony of his esteem and friendship
> for the members of the
> Court of Assistants.
> Geo. Legg, Master,
> Geo. Trust,
> Fredk. Howell, ⎫
> Saml. Wix,   ⎬ Wardens.
> Fredk. Turner, ⎭

---

[1] Vide note 2, page 4.

A handsome ROSEWATER DISH in fine silver (electro deposit), 18 inches in diameter, partly gilt, in the cinque-cento style, with ewer to match, 14 inches in height, elaborately wrought with Neptune, tritons, and sea monsters; weight 68 oz., 1848. The original, from which the above is a facsimile, is in the possession of the Corporation of Norwich.

A large ROSEWATER DISH in fine silver (electro deposit), partly gilt, 18 inches in diameter, elaborately wrought in the Raphaelesque style round the border with figures and devices emblematic of the arts and sciences, in the centre with enrichments representing the four seasons: weight 42 oz., Æ, 1849. The original by Briot, a predecessor of Cellini, is at the Hotel Cluni at Paris.

A SILVER SNUFF-BOX in form of an oval vase, surmounted with the Company's crest, with supporters on either side holding shields engraved with the Company's arms and motto or ribband, the whole mounted on an ebony stand; weight 27 oz. ℔ 1863.

Around the lid there is the following inscription:

Presented to the Worshipful Company of Skinners by Geo. Legg, Esq. in testimony of the kindness of the Wardens, Court of Assistants, and Clerk during his Mastership, June 1863.

SILVER CIGAR-STAND, with supporters of Company, arms and motto:

Presented to the Worshipful Company of Skinners,
George Trist, Master, 1863.

A JEWELLED BADGE in cinque-cento style, of somewhat oval form, richly set with rubies and diamonds; at the base a circular shield surrounded by diamonds, with the date of the Company's charter in enamel. The greater part of the badge is occupied by the arms and supporters in their proper heraldic colours, surmounted by the crest.

On the back is engraved the following inscription:

1874.
Charles Barry,
Master,
Joseph Causton,
Thomas Hobson,
Richard Knight Causton,
William K. L. Langridge,
Wardens.

BARGE-MASTER'S BADGE: shield of the Company in repoussée, laurel-leaved border 10 by 7 inches; weight 18 oz.; date 1719.

The SILVER HEADS to the BEADLE'S STAVES, 14½ inches high, weight 74 oz., the stem and bowl richly embossed, and having on the top the arms, supporters, and crest of the Company.

With regard to the plate I find the somewhat singular entry in the Court Books: " Josiah Colebroke by his will, 1775, bequeathed to the Company two octagon silver candlesticks with silver nozzles, belonging to his late father, on condition that they would also accept and hang two pictures, of his brother and sister, which the Company refused to do."

Some curious and ancient pieces of plate appear to have been disposed of by the Master and Wardens in 1827 by an order of the Court; they are mentioned as follows:

        Two silver tankards, marked R. M.
        One salt stand, the gift of R. Meredith.
        Two   ditto   ditto   John Frewin.
        One   ditto   ditto   Robert Dickinson.
        One   ditto   ditto   Nathl. Wright.
        Four taper candlesticks.
            Also 7 soup ladles.
                12 gravy spoons.
                14 sauce ladles.
                6 sugar-tongs.

At the same time new plate was purchased.

www.ingramcontent.com/pod-product-compliance
Lightning Source LLC
Chambersburg PA
CBHW020134170426
43199CB00010B/744